Writings on the English Civil War

Three Kingdoms Torn Apart

Barry Vale

Also available from Amazon Kindle Publishing:

A History of the Church of England 1529 – 1662

A Brief Study of British Defence Policy

Barry's British History Blogs Compilation

Is Jaguar Land Rover Capable of Global Expansion?

Mythology vs Modernity

Public Diplomacy in Western Democracies

The Augustan Building Programme

The Influence of Changing Gender Roles during the 18th and 19th centuries on the position of women in midwifery

Contents

Preface

Introduction

Section 1

Stability in England – the Stuarts enter the Promised Land

How change and continuity in Early Modern England were reflected in perceptions of crime and social control

Section 2

The Causes of War and Conflict in the Three Kingdoms

An evaluation of the relative importance of short term and long term issues in precipitating the English civil wars.

Section 3

The significance of the passing of the Self Denying Ordinance in 1644 for the outcome of the wars

Section 4

The Treatment of Prisoners of War during the English Civil Wars

The way in which the civil war affected the Guilds of Chester

Section 5

Hobbes & Locke on the State of Nature

Section 6

Outcomes of the English Civil Wars and Leading Figures

Preface

The tradition among British historians has been to call the series of wars that took place in Great Britain and Ireland in the mid 17th century the English Civil Wars. This is many respects is misleading as fighting took place in all of the Three Kingdoms (England, Scotland and Ireland) plus the Principality of Wales that were ruled over by the Stuart dynasty. In theory the entire British Isles been ruled by the same dynasty should have brought strength and unity yet instead it brought war and chaos.

The different sections of this book will explore the causes of the British wars, and the consequences of the conflicts. Although the monarchy was eventually restored the Three Kingdoms would never be the same again.

Introduction

The English Civil Wars are generally described as starting at Edgehill in Warwickshire in October 1642 yet conflict began earlier than that battle. Charles I had proved that he found it really difficult to rule over the Three Kingdoms of England (including Wales), Ireland and Scotland. Charles was unwilling to compromise with his opponents, though none of the parties involved would have wanted to go through the conflicts that beset the Three Kingdoms.

The background and causes of the conflicts are evaluated as well as other aspects including how the New Model Army was created, and how the Royalists were defeated. Charles continued his father's advocacy of the Devine Right of Kings yet lacked the sense, charisma or the ability to induce either fear or loyalty that most of his Tudor predecessors had. Charles, had been James VI / I's second son and his father did not teach him as much about kingship as had been taught to Prince Henry. May be James teaching his son when to compromise could have been just as important as any other teachings about how to govern.

Charles was not the only person at fault for the conflicts that brought untold carnage to the British Isles though his failings as a monarch arguably did not help the situation. In the end the great irony of these bloody conflicts was that the monarchy would return, albeit on terms set by the English Parliament.

Section 1

Stability in England – the Stuarts enter the Promised Land

How change and continuity in Early Modern England were reflected in perceptions of crime and social control

Early Modern England was a country that seemed to be highly conscious of the issues surrounding crime and social control. In many respects England during this period went through profound religious, social, economic and political changes that affected crime and social control. Throughout the Early Modern period however the government with the social and economic elite plus the religious establishment wished to keep crime down to a minimum whilst maintaining the maximum levels of social control. Crime and social control were linked as the means to reduce or counter crime were similar or the same as the methods used for maintaining social control. The government it must be remembered had no standing army or police force to maintain social control and counter crime, so it would have to rely on local militias, mercenaries or the support of members of the nobility if or when needed. As will be examined and discussed below changes and also the continuities of the Early Modern period affected crime and the maintaining of social control. Religion played an important role in the way in which certain actions were considered to be immoral as well as forming some of the foundations needed for effective social control.

In Early Modern England the main methods of reducing and punishing crime were through the clerical, civil and crown courts with the monarch through Parliament or by royal decree being able to change the law. The system had been that way for around four centuries although the Reformation would affect the roles of clerical courts and Parliament. The importance of an effective monarch had been demonstrated by the breakdown in law and order caused by the minority of Henry VI and the disruption caused by the War of the Roses. On some occasions juries were bribed or threatened into acquitting criminals that were supported by or connected to local nobility or merchants. The most powerful families maintained their own private armies and believed that they and their entourages were above the law. Henry VII succeeded in restoring royal authority and the criminal justice system.[1] Crime was undoubtedly considered a major social problem in the Early Modern period although it is not entirely straightforward to compile entirely accurate figures about the level of crime. Courts did keep records of those that were sentenced or acquitted yet there must have been crimes that were not reported and criminals that remained unpunished. If the crime figures are more accurate then Early Modern England saw higher levels of crime than in the preceding and succeeding periods despite social control been stronger than before. [2]

Social control came via the religious and moral teachings of the church, the clerical, civil and crown courts plus the Justices of the Peace that carried out the royal will and punished criminals. The clerical courts could pass judgements and verdicts on religious crimes and serious moral misconduct yet had to revert heresy cases to the crown if they wished to enforce the death penalty. The nobility believed that their rights were enshrined in the Magna Carta although they should not be regarded as being rights for ordinary people. [3] Ultimately it was the monarch that decided the level of social control they considered necessary to ensure that England was secure. The church could provide the monarch with moral and spiritual guidance as well as a means of providing social control. The Tudor monarchs were great believers in using Parliament to recognise, enforce and increase their power. They also recognised that both the House of Lords and the House of Commons contained

---

[1] Elton, 1991 pp. 4-6

[2] Gardiner & Wenborn, 1995 p.211

[3] Lockyer, 1989 p.39

the people most concerned with maintaining social control, those that held property. [4]

The punishments for crimes were often severe, with hundreds of different capital offences yet that did not seem to stop crimes being committed. Judges were often keen to pass capital sentences in order to deter further crime, although poverty as much as poor morals often pushed people towards committing crimes. The main crimes that would nearly always result in the death penalty were murder, rape, theft, serious assault, treason and heresy. The method of execution could depend on the nature of the crime and the social status of the criminal. For instance the wealthy tended to be beheaded, the poorest were hung, heretics got burnt at the stake and traitors were hung, drawn and quartered. [5]

In the Early Modern period there were concerns about declining morality even before the Reformation began. The English church and its clergy although not perfect, apparently had fewer problems with morality than its continental and Irish counterparts. [6]

There were also some legal loopholes that the governments of this period attempted to reduce, such as gaining sanctuary when been inside a church. As a rule the government was content to allow the courts to deal with criminals and would only intervene when it considered acts or crimes to be a threat to social control or a treat to the government's security. Serious breakdowns in social control would prove not to be so frequent as ordinary crimes. Yet such breakdowns were greatly feared by English governments and were usually crushed with great severity. Breakdowns in social control were caused by various social, economic, religious and political factors. Government policies could cause or contribute to such

---

[4] Elton, 1991 pp. 19-20

[5] Gardiner & Wenborn, 1995 p.130

[6] Scarisbrick, 1984 pp. 49-50

breakdowns in social control that were frequently against change rather than in favour of it. For instance the dissolution of the monasteries prompted the Pilgrimage of Grace in order to reverse Henry VIII religious policies. Through appeals to loyalty and broken promises of pardons Henry VIII and the Duke of Norfolk got the rebels to disband. Then they had the ringleaders executed as a demonstration of the fatal consequences of rebelling against the government. The king had told Norfolk to provide false pledges of "free pardon and Parliament" to regain social control.[7]

Aside from the Pilgrimage of Grace the dissolution of the monasteries faced little resistance. The sale of monastic lands increased government revenue and meant that those that brought land were committed to the government's religious changes. The dissolution of the monasteries could have been regarded to have some impact on crime as people that may have been given relief by monasteries may have had to beg or steal to survive, both considered as serious crimes in Early Modern England. [8]

Henry VIII did not pursue any radical Protestant doctrines, and was content to have Roman Catholics that did not accept the Royal Supremacy executed alongside radical Protestants that believed that the Reformation in England had not gone far enough. As far as the government was concerned the moral teachings of the church still had to be observed whether it was Catholic or reformed. Henry was not interested in radical reform for its own sake and rather more interested in maintaining the greater power that the break with Rome had given him. Thomas Cromwell and Thomas Cranmer slowly promoted Protestant reforms. Both men wanted religious reform endorsed by the government to maintain order and social control. Thomas Cromwell did not survive losing Henry VIII's favour whilst Archbishop Cranmer was only able to carry out a more radical reformation in Edward VI's reign. [9]

---

[7]   Kerr, 1990 p.87

[8] Chadwick, 1990 pp. 108-09

The reign of the child Edward VI ushered in an era of regency government with his uncle Edward Seymour becoming Lord Protector. War and economic recession made the social and economic conditions less favourable for social control and forced more people towards crime. Protector Somerset wished to remove the visual and ritual remnants of Roman Catholicism in England. He therefore ordered the closure of the chantries and the removal of Roman Catholic images and statues. Whilst the majority of Protestants adopted these changes such changes threatened social control in more conservative areas like Yorkshire, Lancashire and the south-west. Somerset also raised the hopes of the poor that he would introduce social and economic reforms. [10]

Thomas Cranmer had been unable to abolish the Latin Mass during Henry VIII reign yet had produced the first Book of Common Prayer by 1549. Brought in by the Act of Uniformity the prayer book was unpopular in conservative areas of the country was a major factor in causing rebellions in the West Country and Norfolk. Cranmer had not liked the 1549 prayer book because it was too conservative, for the rebels it was too radical. [11]

The moderate nature of the first prayer book did not prevent it from threatening the breakdown of social control. The economic downturn of the 1540s had produced higher levels of poverty than normal and influenced Parliament into passing the most draconian Poor Laws of the 16th century. The poor were unhappy with the enclosure of farm and common lands for the raising of sheep, it was a constant grievance that remained throughout good times and lean times. Protector Somerset promised to stop enclosures yet although ineffective his promises slackened social control. Protests against enclosures may have been illegal yet they were not unpopular or considered unjustified by the population as a whole. Such crimes

---

[9] Schama, 2000 p. 307

[10] Morgan, 1993 pp. 295-96

[11] Chadwick, 1990 p. 118

have often been described by historians, as social crimes as they were committed to promote social good rather than personal gain. [12]

Enclosures were difficult to stop legally as many of the landlords that made such changes were either Justices of the Peace, MPs, or were close to such people in their social and economic interests. The most serious threat to the government and social control was centred on Norwich and was led by Robert Kett. [13]

Kett and his followers believed that they were upholding religious, social and economic traditions and rights whilst the government were the ones that were either carrying out morally repulsive changes or allowing the rich and powerful to do so. The riots and rebellions of 1549 were "the culmination of this sporadic and spontaneous movement" against social and economic changes imposed from above. [14]

The other rising in Devon and Cornwall had only been crushed after a month long siege of Exeter. That was followed by the death of around 4,000 rebels once government forces caught up with them at Samford Courtenay. Kett's rebellion was a more serious threat to the government and its ability to maintain social control. Protector Somerset's inability to crush that rebellion led to his replacement by the more competent Earl of Warwick. Warwick had ruthlessly crushed the Kett rebellion with German mercenaries. Warwick promoted himself to Duke of Northumberland and tried to subvert the succession of Mary Tudor in order to save the Protestant Reformation and save his own skin in the process. That was something that no rebel had tried to do in 1549.[15]

Arguably the government's obsession with maintaining tight social controls and trying to enforce religious conformity could backfire.

---

[12] Gardiner & Wenborn, 1995 p. 701

[13] Gardiner & Wenborn, 1995 p. 701

[14] Elton, 1991 pp. 206-07

[15] Schama, 2000 pp. 321-22

For instance, Mary Tudor had at first been popular yet her persecution of the Protestants and her marriage to Phillip of Spain prompted the Wyatt Rebellion that was a greater threat to the safety of Princess Elizabeth than Queen Mary herself.[16] Given time and an heir Mary's restoration of Roman Catholicism may have succeeded despite Protestant propaganda. However the predetermined persecution of hundreds of Protestants as heretics made many of their compatriots regard them as martyrs rather than subversive criminals.[17] Elizabeth I only faced one rebellion in England during her long reign, the Northern Rising of 1569. That rebellion was ineptly led and ineffectively organised by Lord Darcy and the Duke of Northumberland and its military threat would prove insignificant. The rising did succeed in inducing panic in the government fearing that it could succeed in placing Mary Queen of Scots onto the throne. Elizabeth ordered the execution of 700 rebels to show that rebellions would not succeed and that involvement in them was foolish, although if she had ordered the execution of Mary Queen of Scots she would have saved herself a lot of trouble.[18] A consequence of the Northern Rising was that the Pope issued a bull excommunicating Elizabeth and calling for her removal from the English throne. That bull created a dilemma for Catholics of whether to obey the Pope or remain loyal subjects of the Queen. It is allowed the government to treat radical Catholics and missionary priests sent from Europe as traitors and have them executed.[19]

The Stuarts inadvertently changed the balance of the English constitution and legal system. James I insisted upon the divine right of kings and argued with Parliament and leading lawyers such as Sir Edward Coke over the royal prerogative to raise taxes and make legal decisions. James argued that kings were above the law, whilst Coke countered that not even kings were above English common

---

[16] Starkey, 2001, p.140

[17] Ivory, Weston et al, 2002 p.65

[18] Fletcher & MacCulloch, 1997 p. 102

[19] MacCulloch, 1990, p.145

law.[20] James I declared that he liked common law as it was "favourable and advantageous for a king" to use it to maintain his power and status.[21]

There was perhaps one set of sentences that Coke passed, which James would not have disagreed with. He condemned the Gunpowder Plotters to death and made everybody aware of the significance of having traitors hung, drawn and quartered.[22] The government's ability to effectively maintain social controls was undermined by the disputes between Charles I and Parliament that led to the English Civil War and eventually a constitutional monarchy that protected the interests of the rich and powerful more effectively than before.[23]

Early Modern England did seem to have a problem with crime if not social control. It would be unrealistic to believe that any country could totally eradicate crime or the need for some form or level of social control. In a sense Early Modern England witnessed a return to tighter social control once the Tudor dynasty was secure and the instability of the Wars of the Roses became a thing of the past. Law was based on the clerical, civil and Crown courts with Parliament passing legislation and the monarch being the final arbiter. Social control was based on the social and economic order, the teachings of the church, the effectiveness of the courts and the power of the Crown. The Reformation, imposed as it was from above altered the balance between the Crown, Parliament and the church. The church was the loser whilst the enhanced power of the Crown would bring it conflict with Parliament at the end of the Early Modern period. Crime did not go away during this period and most evidence suggests that it actually increased. The courts tried to deter crime by passing the harshest sentences available to them. Economic necessity

---

[20] Schama, 2001 p.27

[21] Lockyer, 1989 p. 59

[22] Ivory, Weston et al, 2002 p. 103

[23] Schama, 2001 p. 244

rather than the moral failings of those that committed them drove most crime. The period did see high inflation and some bad harvests that affected the poorest the hardest. Some believed that their actions were morally justified such as stopping enclosures or trying to reverse the course of the Reformation. All the rebellions that broke out during this period were crushed without too much difficulty. At the end of this period it was not petty criminals that broke the social control of the government. It was some of the MPs, the Justices of the Peace and the gentry that wished to change the economic, religious and social policies of the government that brought civil war with a king too convinced of his own divine right to back down.

Perhaps what made maintaining law and order as well as political stability for Charles I was keeping order in Scotland as well as the rest of the British Isles. For a variety of reasons Charles managed to alienate enough people to undermine his control of all of his kingdoms. Unfortunately for him enough of the rich and powerful reached the conclusion that his policies needed to be overturned and that he could not remain in power.

Bibliography

Chadwick (1990) The Penguin History of the Church 3 – the Reformation 2nd edition, Penguin, London

Elton GR (1991) England under the Tudors 3rd edition, Routledge, London

Fletcher & MacCulloch (1997) Tudor Rebellions 4th edition, Addison Wesley Longman Limited, London

Gardiner J & Wenborn N (1995) The History Today Companion to British History, Collins & Brown, London

Ivory M, Weston H, Nation M, Williams M, Bagshaw C, Kinnaird D & Taylor H (2002) Bloody Britain – A history of murder, mayhem and massacre, AA publishing, Windsor

Kerr (1990) The Penguin Book of Lies, Viking, London

Lockyer R (1989) The Early Stuarts – A political History of England 1603 – 1642, Longman, London and New York

MacCulloch D (1990) The Later Reformation in England 1547-1603, Macmillan, Basingstoke

Morgan K O (1993) The Oxford Popular History of Britain, Oxford University Press, Oxford

Scarisbrick J J (1984) The Reformation and the English People

Schama S (2000) A History of Britain 1 – At the edge of the world 3000 BC – 1603 AD, BBC Worldwide, London

Schama S (2001) A History of Britain 2 – The British Wars 1603-1776, BBC Worldwide, London

Starkey D (2001) Elizabeth, Vintage, London

Section 2 The Causes of War and Conflict in the Three Kingdoms

An evaluation of the relative importance of short term and long term issues in precipitating the English civil wars.

The following section will evaluate the relative importance of short and long term issues in precipitating the English Civil Wars. Undoubtedly, the English Civil Wars was caused by a mixture of both short term and long term issues that eventually led to the outbreak of fighting during the later months of 1642. Short term and long term issues were related to constitutional, religious, political, and economic events, developments, and beliefs. These events, developments, and beliefs that contributed to the outbreak of conflict were not just confined to England, but were also linked to issues relating to Scotland and Ireland that were influential upon English / Welsh developments and issues. The way in which short term and long term issues combined to cause the English Civil War are arguably complex and have provided the opportunity for a great deal of historical debate.

The long term issues that helped to precipitate the English Civil War were important in shaping the actions, beliefs, and policies of those people and groups that actually brought the conflict into fruition.[24] Some of the long term issues discussed here had been potential or actual problems for many decades, yet it took influence from short term issues to make long term issues destructive of peace and stability within the three kingdoms ruled by Charles I.[25] As the monarch of three kingdoms Charles I theoretically held a great deal of power and status. Reality was different, for Charles was faced with difficulties and constraints within all his possessions.[26] To some extent Charles' predecessors had managed, contained, or

---

[24] Ashton, 1978

[25] Bennet, 1997 p. 4

[26] Kishlansky, 2005, also Royale 2004 p.14

simply ignored long term issues, yet issues left on the back burner had not been solved and just needed the emergence of short term issues to act as catalysts to precipitate the English Civil Wars.[27]

Like his father and the Tudors before him, Charles found that controlling his realms was hampered by a lack of money and resources. If the monarch avoided going to war they could just about get by financially without calling Parliaments to grant taxes and subsidies. However, to do so the monarch would have to raise their own taxes, subsidies, or persuade their subjects to lend them money. Those options were not always particularly effective and certainly were not politically advisable.[28]

The Tudors had been effective managers of Parliament, yet even they had not been able to gain enough taxes and subsidies to become financially self-sufficient. Such self-sufficiency would have reduced the need for and importance of Parliament.[29] Potentially the dissolution of the monasteries could have allowed the Crown to be free of the need for Parliamentary taxes. Henry VIII sold most of those assets to buy support for his religious changes, and for defences against the risk of invasion.[30]

Financial weakness meant that the Crown had to resort to calling Parliaments out of necessity instead of constitutional obligations. Parliament's influence if not its power had increased as a result of passing the legislation for the break from Rome, and members eventually realised the government could be influenced, or prepared to make concessions to have legislation passed.[31] The Crown needed Parliament to make its policies more effective. Parliament generally accepted the policies of the Tudors, yet its members had a strong

---

[27] Ashton, 1978

[28] Kishlansky, 1996 p. 120

[29] Smith, 1999 p. 20

[30] Vale, 2006 p. 53

[31] Smith, 1999 p. 20

sense of their constitutional rights and importance. Elizabeth I's moderation had prevented any serious rift, yet the Stuarts were not ones to back down. The long term issue of Parliament's position and privileges was one that did not fade away.[32]

The long term issue of the relationship between monarch and Parliament became increasingly likely to provoke conflict once the Stuarts gained control of the English throne. James I was a strong advocate of the divine right of kings, Charles also maintained an unwavering belief in that concept. The problem with the divine right concept was that it undermined the relationship between the monarchy and Parliament, with the monarch less likely to compromise while Parliament wanted to protect its rights and privileges.[33]

Religion was the cause of long term issues that precipitated the English Civil War. The Reformation had profound political, social, economic and religious affects upon the three kingdoms that were ignored with peril.[34] The Church of England was the national church that contained Catholic and Protestant elements, Elizabeth I had not enforced strict conformity to maintain political stability. The future of the English Church was an issue that could cause controversy if not sensibly discussed or managed. Furthermore, the Stuarts had to consider the importance of religion in keeping things stable in Ireland and Scotland.[35]

In Scotland religious matters reflected the weakness of the monarchy in relation to the fiercely Calvinist Church of Scotland clergy and congregations, the monarchy also had to endure powerful nobles. James I had tried to gain control over the Scots Church yet had not pushed things too quickly due to royal interference being bitterly

---

[32] Ashley, 2002 p. 251

[33] Royale, 2004 p. 14

[34] Schama, 2001 p. 87

[35] Vale, 2006 p. 46

resented. On the other hand, Charles decided to make conservative changes without consulting anybody first.[36]

In Ireland the population had remained overwhelmingly Roman Catholic and resistant to English rule.[37] Ireland had been a long term issue in its own right before the Reformation, the addition of a religious element to the situation made the potential for causing conflict even greater.[38] Elizabeth I had been confronted by a major rebellion in Ulster, and James I resorted to settling Protestant plantations in that province to increase loyalty to the Crown.[39]

Ireland was an issue that always seemed to cause concern with the English government, sometimes it might seem to be stable but the fear of Irish rebellion remained strong.[40]

Another long term issue that contributed to the outbreak of the English Civil War was arguments about the relative rights of subjects in their obligations towards the Crown and church. This was more of a long term issue in England than in Ireland or Scotland, in the sense that the English political and economic elites had a greater sense of what the government could or could not do.[41]

Whilst the Tudors had increased the powers of the Crown as a result of the implementation of religious changes, they had been careful to maintain the loyalty of both the nobility and the gentry. Perhaps the best indication of how good the relationship between the monarchy and its wealthiest subjects was reflected in the attitudes of Parliament. Parliament's role went beyond passing legislation and

---

[36] Kishlansky, 1996 p. 132

[37] Ashton, 1978, see also MacCulloch, 2004 p. 397

[38] Bennet, 1997 p.4)

[39] MacCulloch, 2004 p. 397

[40] Kishlansky,1996 p. 146

[41] Smith, 1999, p.27

approving taxation, it was a barometer of public opinion, and it allowed grievances to be heard. Alongside the monarch, Parliament determined what was legal and constitutional, good relations between them allowed England to be governed more effectively.[42]

The main area of contention was whether Crown or Parliament had the final say when there was no consensus over an issue. Traditionally the monarchy had the most power, yet the concept of the divine right of kings openly proclaimed by the Stuarts disturbed the balance between the Crown and the political and economical elites represented by Parliament. Parliament would eventually believe it had to confront the king to protect its own position.[43]

The short term issues were essential to the precipitation of the English Civil War, without them the long term issues may not have provided enough impetus to start the conflict under their own auspices. The majority of the short term issues were directly linked to the personality and the policies of Charles I.[44] James I had made sure that his son was heavily influenced by the concept of the divine right of kings, which may not have been so detrimental had Charles known when to compromise. He liked order and conformity, whilst disliking opposition to his policies and plans.[45]

The unwillingness to listen to criticism or tolerate opposition meant that Charles was determined to rule without Parliament after opposition at the start of his reign.[46] For such a strategy to work effectively Charles needed to raise as much revenue as possible to avoid wars against foreign countries and if possible avoiding political, economic or religious crisis within his realms. The strategy of ruling without Parliament would fail due to the government's

---

[42] Smith, 199, p.20)

[43] Royale, 2004 p. 160

[44] Schama, 2001 p. 86

[45] Lockyer, 1989 p. 218

[46] Ashton, 1978

inability to manage, or contain other short term issues. The majority of English and Scottish subjects paid their levies, feudal dues, and taxes without much protest, although the issues of taxation without representation provided an opportunity for opponents to protest against Charles' personal rule.[47]

Charles did not seem to understand the political damage un-parliamentary taxation raised by such methods allowed his government to function and brought benefits like a stronger Royal Navy, and greater stability in Ireland without the inconvenience of having to put up with a moaning parliament. The government tried to strictly enforce the tax and revenue collections by force, cajoling and through the law courts. Most infamously, the government decided to collect 'ship money' to pay for the rejuvenated Royal Navy in counties across the whole of England and Wales, instead of just coastal counties (Schama, 2001 p. 84). The issues over taxation helped to increase the opposition to Charles I in Scotland, as well as in England.[48]

If Charles' handling of taxation issues was bad, his handling of religious issues proved to be truly inept. In diplomatic and dynastic terms his marriage to Henrietta Maria of France had been a sensible match. However, in terms of preventing religious issues undermining political stability, it proved to be the start of Charles' downfall. Protestant opinion in England and Scotland was dismayed that Henrietta Maria was allowed to remain a Roman Catholic and bring a large contingent of catholic clergy with her.[49]

Charles did not share his Protestant subjects' prejudices and rabid fears of Catholicism, which helps to explain why he failed to anticipate the fierce opposition that his religious policies caused in England and Scotland. Legally Charles was entitled to have a great deal of control over the English and Scots national churches,

---

[47] Lockyer, 1989 p. 230)

[48] Kishlansky, 1996 p.120

[49] Coward, 1994, p. 160

crucially he lacked the sense to know when it was wise to change things or to leave things as they were.[50] Charles' poor decision-making over religious issues was made worse by William Laud's influence and advice. Laud was against the Puritan elements within the Church of England, like Charles he wished to increase the level of conformity by purging Puritan clergy and practices.[51] These policies provoked opposition from radical Protestants that were well placed to cause trouble in England and Scotland, whose propaganda against Charles was effective in gaining support.[52]

The decision to introduce a Prayer Book into Scotland was disastrous as it provoked fierce opposition. The Scots were prepared to fight their king to defend their church. The issue over the Prayer Book led to the Bishop's War. The Scots resistance, forcing Charles to call Parliament to pay for a new army easily defeated the English Army. The Scots won both of the Bishop's Wars, whilst Charles did not want to agree to the demands of the Long Parliament.[53]

He was forced to accept the trial and execution of Strafford. It was Strafford's removal from Ireland that led to the Irish rebellion. The need to crush that rebellion led to much argument between Charles and the Parliament over control of the army to be sent to Ireland. Parliament was highly sceptical of Charles' motives and therefore wanted to gain control of the army.[54] In the end no English army was raised to go to Ireland, a Scots army went instead, paid for by the English Parliament yet controlling itself.[55] Charles was not overly concerned about losing control of the army as he believed the strong support for him outside of London would prove sufficient to win the

---

[50] Kishlansky, 1996 p. 132

[51] Schama, 2001 p. 86

[52] Kishlansky, 2005

[53] Kishlansky, 1996 p.132

[54] Lockyer, 1989 p. 359

[55] Royale, 2004 p. 141

civil war, whilst having the Scots fighting in Ireland was to his advantage.[56]

Therefore, a combination of short and long term issues precipitated the English Civil War. Long term issues had made the possibility of civil war or serious disturbances likely, yet they did not make conflict inevitable. Long term issues were important as they determined the beliefs, attitudes, and actions of the people that brought about the English Civil War. Long term issues such as the relationship between the monarchy and Parliament, the importance of religious beliefs, or the monarchy's shortage of money and its means of raising taxes without Parliamentary consent made conflict probable.

However, it was short term issues that started the conflict. Charles I managed to alienate too many people with his policies, ruling without Parliament and raising unpopular taxes made him unpopular with social and economic elites as well as religious groups that were able to mobilise opposition against him. Attempting to impose a Prayer Book on the Scots was foolish and provoked the Bishop's War. The Bishop's War was important as it forced the calling of Parliament. Parliament clashed with Charles as to the control of the army to fight with the Scots and was aggrieved about his belief in the divine right of kings taking precedence over their privileges. The Irish Rebellion intensified the divisions and just about made the English Civil War inevitable. Fear of Catholicism and mistrust of Charles meant that Parliament was unwilling to back down, whilst Charles was too stubborn to compromise.

---

[56] Young, 1997 p. 208

Bibliography

Ashley M, (2002) A brief history of British Kings & Queens, Robinson, London
Ashton R, (1978) The English Civil War, Weidenfeld & Nicholson, London
Bennet M, (1998) The Civil Wars 1637 –53
Coward B, (1994) The Stuart Age – England 1603 - 1714, Pearson Education Limited, London
Kishlansky M, (1996) A Monarchy Transformed 163 – 1714, Penguin Books, London
Kishlansky M, (2005) Charles 1: a case of mistaken identity past and present
Lockyer R, (1989) The Early Stuarts A Political History of England, Longman Group Limited, London
MacCulloch D, Reformation – Europe's House Divided (2004) Penguin Books, London
Royale T, (2006) Civil War – The Wars of the Three Kingdoms 1638 – 1660, Abacus, London
Schama S, (2001) A History of Britain - The British Wars 1603-1776, BBC Worldwide, London
Smith D L (1999) The Stuart Parliaments 1603 – 1689, Arnold Publishing, London
Vale B, (2006) A History of the Church of England 1529 – 1662, Amazon Kindle
Young M B, (1997) Charles I

Section 3

The significance of the passing of the Self Denying Ordinance in 1644 for the outcome of the wars

Outlined below is a discussion of how significant the passing of the Self Denying Ordinance in 1644 was in relation to subsequent political and military events. The Self Denying Ordinance was passed amidst the backdrop of the English Civil War, which in turn affected its objectives and its actual significance. The Self Denying Ordinance was drawn up by the Long Parliament during 1644 in an effort to reduce its considerable divisions over how its armies and militias were organised and fighting in the first English Civil War. As will be discussed and evaluated the divisions amongst the two main factions within Parliament were the debates concerning the over all objectives for fighting, and also the strategies needed to win the English Civil War. The passing of the Self Denying Ordinance in 1644 was intended solely to allow Parliament to go on to gain victory over the royalists, arguably it served its purpose yet perhaps not in the ways it was intended to do so. The original intention of the Self Denying Ordinance was that no peer or Member of Parliament (MP) could hold a commission in the Parliamentary army and navy. Only carefully selected members would be considered to become officers in the New Model Army and the New Model Navy.

When the English Civil War began in October 1642 the Parliamentary and royalist forces were fairly evenly matched yet the greater resources available to Parliament meant they should have been winning the war. [57] Parliament had a greater share of tax revenues, found it easier to raise loans, controlled the London militias (and therefore the city), held the majority of naval ports, as well as the navy. Controlling the ports and the navy was important as it meant that the royalists found it harder to gain money and supplies from abroad.[58] When Parliament made an alliance with the

---

[57]Carlin, 1999 p. 31

[58]Fraser, 1973 p. 120; Poulson, 1984 p. 78

Scottish Presbyterian armies then considered to be the most effective soldiers in the British Isles many felt that this alliance should lead to victory sooner rather than later.[59] Radical elements in Parliament regarded the Self Denying Ordinance as the key measure to allow them to take full advantage of these favourable factors.[60]

At the start of the English Civil War the main Parliamentary army commanders had been the Earls of Essex and Manchester who were inexperienced at holding such commands, unlike the commanders of the Scottish Presbyterian armies or the royalist cavalry commander Prince Rupert of the Rhine.[61] Not only were the Earls of Essex and Manchester inexperienced, they were generally cautious in their tactics and were half-hearted in their desire to defeat the king, and would have accepted peace offers, if Charles I had offered these to them. To the annoyance of the more radical elements within the Parliamentary forces the Earls of Essex and Manchester had been prepared to accept all the conditions set by the Scottish Presbyterians without exception.[62] Had the Earls of Essex of Manchester remained in charge of English Parliamentary forces that the Scottish would have had a greater influence over subsequent events, and that the New Model Army would not have fought them.[63] The Self Denying Ordinance would shift the balance of power in the English Parliamentary and Scottish Presbyterian alliance in favour of the radicals within the Parliamentary forces, though that was not predicted in 1644 or 1645.[64]

The Self Denying Ordinance suited those radicals in the

---

[59] Royale, 2004 p.169

[60] Hill, 1980 p. 108

[61] Fraser, 1973 p. 17

[62] Royale, 2004 p. 184

[63] Ashley, 1977 p. 39

[64] Schama, 2001 p. 230

Parliamentary forces that wanted to gain complete control of these armies to win the English Civil War.[65] There were radical critics of the Earls of Essex and Manchester most notably Oliver Cromwell and Henry Ireton who claimed that their ill-suited commanders' tactics, strategies, and uninspiring leadership were more likely to lead to defeat rather than victory.[66] For instance, if the royalist commanders especially Prince Rupert had led their troops better at the Battle of Edge Hill they could have reached London. A successful assault on London would have meant that the English Civil War would have ended almost as soon as it had begun.[67] Cromwell and Ireton wanted the Self-Denying Ordinance so that they could make the Earls of Essex and Manchester give up their commissions within the Parliamentary armies. The House of Lords were also reluctant to pass the ordinance. Cromwell was its most ardent advocate as it was the only way to avoid "a dishonourable peace".[68] The Earl of Manchester suspected that its passing would fill the Parliamentary armies "Anabaptists and sectaries, a breed of people who would do away with titles and privileges and were potential regicides".[69]

The Earls of Essex and Manchester were not initially happy to accept the Self-Denying Ordinance, and only agreed to it as they understood that the ordinance meant Oliver Cromwell and Henry Ireton along with the more radical MPs within the Parliamentary armies would lose their commissions as well.[70] The moderates assumed that these radicals would not give up their seats in the House of Commons to retain their rank in the army, and so would have to resign from the army.[71] The moderate elements within

---

[65] Smith 1997 p. 323

[66] Royale, 2004 p. 169

[67] Fraser, 1973 p. 60

[68] Royale, 2004 p. 311

[69] Royale, 2004 p. 310

[70] Schama, 2001 p. 231

parliament were opposed to the Self Denying Ordinance and a second version had to be developed to finally gain support for the purging of the officers of the Parliamentary armies. Cromwell showed he was as astute at politics as he was fighting in a battle.[72] The removal of the Earls of Essex and Manchester from military command was therefore the first significant consequence of the passing of the Self-Denying Ordinance in 1644.[73]

The passing of the Self Denying Ordinance in 1644 was significant because it ended the impasse within the Parliamentary armies and Parliament about the best tactics and strategies to be pursued in order to win the English Civil War. The moderate as well as the radical elements on the Parliamentary side accepted with varying degrees of enthusiasm the passing of the Self-Denying Ordinance in order to develop coherent tactics and strategies to defeat the royalists.[74] The leaders of the Parliamentary armies realised that too many arguments about tactics and strategies would be seriously counter-productive, and would also allow the royalist to recovering from their shattering defeat at the Battle of Marston Moor.[75] Oliver Cromwell was the Parliamentary commander that emerged from the victory at Marston Moor with the most prestige, with his cavalry regiment of Ironsides being a highly effective unit. Cromwell could potentially have lost the most from the passing of the Self-Denying Ordinance in 1644.[76] Instead of losing position and influence within the Parliamentary armies due to the passing of the Self Denying Ordinance, Cromwell actually gained from it been passed. Cromwell though argued that Parliament gained the most, as its armies were no longer "ragged, insubordinate, ill-fed, ill-equipped". [77] After the House of Lords

---

[71]Fraser, 1973 p. 141

[72]Royale, 2004 p. 311

[73]Smith, 1997 p. 322

[74]Bruce & Masson, 1875

[75]Fraser, 1973 p. 128

[76]Young, 1970 p. 123

rejected the first version of the Self Denying Ordinance, Cromwell was specifically exempted from the need to resign his army position by the second version of the ordinance, which was successfully passed through the House of Lords after months of heated discussions. The passing of the Self Denying Ordinance made it possible for the emergence of the New Model Army heavily influenced by Cromwell during the pivotal year of 1645.[78]

The development of, and the subsequent fighting capabilities of the New Model Army and to a lesser extent the New Model Navy were thus significant outcomes of the passing of the Self Denying Ordinance in 1644. Instead of the Parliamentary forces being poorly organised with variable standards of equipment, tactics, strategy, and commanding officers the New Model Army emerged as a very effective fighting force, that went on to defeat all the enemies that it faced.[79] The passing of the Self Denying Ordinance got rid of the amateur, moderate, and faltering leadership of the Earls of Essex and Manchester, whilst allowing Cromwell, Ireton, and Sir Thomas Fairfax to take commands.[80] The newly empowered commanders proceeded to forge the New Model Army into a fighting force that reflected their tactics and strategies as well as their religious and political outlook. The new commanders ensured that the New Model Army was well equipped, well organised, with its troopers been noted for their devotion to the success of the Parliamentary cause.[81] Placing Sir Thomas Fairfax in charge was a sound choice yet Oliver Cromwell was considered by many Parliamentarians and royalists as the lynchpin of the New Model Army that emerged after the passing of the Self Denying Ordinance, and recruited men equally committed to defeating the king into that army.[82] The better

---

[77] Fraser, 1973 p. 143

[78] Hill, 1980 p. 108

[79] Smith, 1997 p. 323

[80] Schama, 2001 p. 231

[81] Fraser, 1973 p. 143

[82] Royale, 2004 p. 312

organisation, equipment, and training thus enabled the New Model Army to overwhelmingly defeat the royalists at the Battle of Naseby The Parliamentary victory at Naseby effectively ended any prospects of the royalists ever winning the English Civil War.[83]

Another significant result of the passing of the Self Denying Ordinance was that it changed the nature of the political and military alliance between the English Parliamentary forces and the Scottish Presbyterian Armies. Before the passing of the Self Denying Ordinance the Scottish Presbyterian Armies had been able to generally persuade the English Parliamentary forces and their political masters to do what they wanted to do. After the passing of the Self Denying Ordinance the domination of the radical and hard line elements meant that the English Parliament in general, and the New Model Army in particular were not content to meekly do everything requested of them by the Scottish Presbyterian Armies.[84] The alliance between the English Parliament and the Scots lasted long enough to ensure final victory over the royalists was won. However the Scots were unhappy that the English Parliament did not keep the promises made to them when the alliance was first agreed to, yet the moderate leadership of the Earls of Essex and Manchester might have stuck to those agreements. Oliver Cromwell and those with similar views did not want the Scots to dictate to them when it came down to the political and religious that they should hold and indeed impose throughout the British Isles. Cromwell also suspected that the Scots just like the Earls of Essex and Manchester would always be ready to reach an agreement with Charles I whenever it would suit them to do so. That suspicion was ultimately vindicated when the Scots attempted to restore Charles I and later Charles II to the throne. As the passing of the Self Denying Ordinance had given Fairfax and Cromwell control of the most potent force in Britain in the form of the New Model Army, they were capable of fighting on until they won whether in alliance with the Scots or fighting against them.[85]

---

[83]Fernandez-Arnesto, & Wilson, 1996, Bantam Press, London

[84]Fraser, 1973 p. 144

There are arguments that the passing of the Self Denying Ordinance in 1644 was not actually as significant as many contemporaries or historians have depicted. The alliance between the English Parliamentary forces and the Scots would probably have won the English Civil War without the passing of the Self Denying Ordinance as the military and naval balance of was strongly in their favour as the royalists were over stretched in maintaining their war effort. The English Parliamentary forces and their Scots allies held the majority of the most strategically important cities or towns including London, Hull, York, and Edinburgh whilst the royalists held a decreasing amount of territory. The English Civil War was a conflict of attrition and all the long-tern factors were in the favour of the Parliamentary forces provided they avoided in catastrophic defeats similar to the one they had inflicted upon the royalists at Marston Moor. The Parliamentary forces were after all in danger of losing that battle until Oliver Cromwell had intervened decisively to turn defeat into victory. As the war dragged on the Parliamentary forces could reinforce their armies with considerably less difficulty than the royalists could theirs. Victory if they remained focused, patient, and united was theirs for the taking, the royalists had rely on the Parliamentary forces making disastrous errors to win the war.[86]

As the royalists lost further amounts of territory it further weakened their chances of finding resources and manpower to continue fighting. After their defeat at Marston Moor the royalists managed to regroup yet their commanders were well aware that they could not match the numerical or material strength of the Parliamentary forces unless they could arrange for reinforcements from the European mainland or Ireland. The queen's connections to the French government were a potential means of gaining enough reinforcements to turn royalist fortunes around, if they could arrive safely in England. The royalist commanders were hoping that the next major battle if they could manage to win it would enhance the prospects of winning the war. The onus was effectively upon the

---

[85]Royale, 2004 p. 312

[86]Fraser, 1973 p. 144

royalists to achieve a spectacular military victory or to convince the Parliamentary forces and their Scots allies to make a peace agreement to end the conflict. Even if the Self Denying Ordinance had not been passed the royalist commanders were aware that they were losing the war and they were reliant upon the Parliamentary forces and the Scots failing to take advantage of the factors that could decisively defeat them to stay involved in the conflict.[87]

Although the royalists had succeeded in capturing the port of Bristol after a successful siege it was not as big a blow to the Parliamentary cause as Charles I had hoped or the Parliamentary military commanders had feared. The over riding problem for the royalists was that had declining amounts of money, weapons, munitions, and fighting men available to continue fighting let alone win the war out right. Capturing Bristol did not resolve such shortages sufficiently enough for the royalist commanders to alter the balance of the conflict in their favour. The royalist ships were not able to bring in supplies in the quantities required as the Parliamentary navy effectively blockaded the major ports of the British mainland. Given enough time even under the command of the excessively cautious Earls of Essex and Manchester the numerical as well the material superiority of the Parliamentary forces would have won the English Civil War. They might not have had needed to fight on to the bitter end as Charles I might have reached a settlement with them to end the war.[88]

The Self Denying Ordinance was not actually necessary in order for the Parliamentary forces to become more effective, and thus win the war. As the most effective and committed of the Parliamentary commanders would have undoubtedly gained a greater influence and even control upon over all military tactics and strategies employed by the Parliamentary forces. He had after all boosted his already rising reputation as a military leader during the victory won at Marston Moor whilst further undermining the position of the Earls of Essex and Manchester. Whilst without the passing of the Self

---

[87]Schama, 2001 p. 231

[88]Royale, 2004 p. 312

Denying Ordinance the Earls of Essex and Manchester would have remained the nominal heads of the English Parliamentary forces the authority they actually exercised would have declined as the hard liners in general and Oliver Cromwell in particular gained prestige for their victories. Naturally enough de facto control of the Parliamentary forces would have passed to these hard liners given enough time. As the Scots representative amongst the Parliamentary forces, Robert Baillie noted the English commanders were "an irresolute, divided, and dangerously –humoured people".[89]

Therefore to conclude there were various significant outcomes that resulted as a consequence of the passing of the Self Denying Ordinance in 1644. The Parliamentary efforts to win the English Civil War before the passing of the Self Denying Ordinance had been faltering due to divisions over tactics, strategies, and the lack of quality in the military leadership. Up to 1644 the main leaders of the Parliamentary forces had been the Earls of Essex and Manchester, and they were indeed perceived as being half-hearted in their approach to the conduct of the war as they would have preferred to have come to terms with the king. The purpose of the passing of the Self Denying Ordinance was to force the moderate commanders out of their positions, and allow the hard liners such as Oliver Cromwell to take their places. After the passing of the Self Denying Ordinance, therefore Oliver Cromwell and Sir Thomas Fairfax were appointed the main commanders of the newly created New Model Army. The emergence of the New Model Army was a politically as well as a militarily significant consequence of the passing of the Self Denying Ordinance for it determined the final outcome of the English Civil War. It was arguably Oliver Cromwell that gained the most from the passing of the Self Denying Ordinance in 1644 as he was the most forceful of the New Model Army commanders, respected by many, and feared by all that subsequently fought against him. In many respects the Self Denying Ordinance was far more of a political necessity than a military one as the longer the war continued the less likely a royalist victory became.

Without the passing of the Self Denying Ordinance it would have

---

[89]Royale, 2004 p. 319

been much harder for Cromwell to achieve his political and military prominence during the Commonwealth and the Lord Protectorate. On the other hand the Earls of Essex and Manchester never held command, but at least they could retire into the background. However it was the monarchy, and the Scottish Presbyterian Armies that were undoubtedly the biggest losers from the passing of the Self Denying Ordinance, Charles I because it cost him his life, Charles II because he had to remain in exile. The Scots were heavily defeated by the New Model Army at Dunbar, Preston, and lastly at Worcester. Under Cromwell and Fairfax (until 1649) the New Model Army was virtually unbeatable and only the inability to find a replacement for Cromwell led to the restoration of the monarchy. Without the passing of the Self Denying Ordinance the New Model Army would not have been so effective, with the Earls of Essex and Manchester still in charge the royalists could have won.

Bibliography

Ashley, M. England in the Seventeenth Century (1977) Oxford University Press, Oxford
Bruce J & Masson D, (1875) The Quarrel between the Earl of Manchester and Oliver Cromwell, Camden Press, London
Carlin, N. Historical Association Studies - The Causes of the English Civil War (1999) Blackwell Publishers Ltd, Oxford.
Fraser A, (1973) Cromwell, Our Chief of Men, Panther Books, London
Hill C, (1980) the Century of Revolution 1603 -1714 2nd edition, Routledge, London
Poulsen, C. the English rebels (1984) The Journeyman Press, London & New York
Royale T, (2004) Civil War - The Wars of the Three Kingdoms, Pimlico, London
Schama S, (2001) A History of Britain - The British Wars 1603-1776, BBC Worldwide, London
Smith A G R, (1997) the Emergence of a Nation State the Commonwealth of England 1529-1660, 2nd edition Longman, London and New York
Young P, (1970) Marston Moor, London

Section 4

The Treatment of Prisoners of War during the English Civil Wars

Contents

Introduction

Chapter One - the treatment of prisoners of war during the first English Civil War

Chapter Two – the treatment of prisoners of war during the second and third English Civil Wars

Conclusions

Introduction

The following is an evaluation of the treatment of prisoners of war during the English Civil Wars between 1642 and 1651. The English Civil Wars took place during an era in which the treatment of prisoners of war did not have any set conventions or legal guidelines that were binding upon all the combatants involved in these conflicts. There were different concepts and contending notions as to how prisoners of war should be treated yet none of the competing sides during the English Civil Wars have to strictly adhere to legally binding ways of dealing with their captives. There were as will discussed in the following chapters and conclusion informal rules and procedures about how wars should or should not be conducted. However there was no single definitive and indeed binding set of rules when it came down to the treatment of prisoners of war.

The concepts that existed before and during the English Civil Wars concerning the fighting of a just war and therefore how prisoners of war and civilians should be treated were open to different interpretations and all sides claimed to be fighting justly.[90] The fact that the English Civil Wars was actually three separate civil wars rather than conflicts between different countries complicated the ways in which prisoners of war were treated. Contemporaries did record how prisoners of war were treated during the English Civil Wars, and some of these accounts will be discussed in the framework of the following evaluation. The contemporary accounts of the treatment of prisoners of war during the English Civil Wars were sometimes used for propaganda purposes, which will be taken into consideration.[91]

During the English Civil Wars the respective combatants did not necessarily regard their captives in the same way or even take prisoners of war in the same circumstances as would be done in

---

[90]MacCulloch, 2004 p. 520

[91]Fraser, 2004 p. 343

modern times. During the English Civil Wars prisoners of war were taken in the midst of or following battles, after the end of sieges or just as an unplanned consequence of being in the wrong place at the wrong time once the fighting had begun. Some prisoners were taken captive because of who they were; they were political prisoners rather than prisoners of war. The most important prisoners of war were more likely to be put upon trial. Conversely less attention was generally paid to the ordinary men simply caught up in the fighting of the English Civil Wars as soldiers were frequently press ganged into the rival armies instead of volunteering to fight for their preferred cause, as many would have preferred to stay neutral. Indeed all the armies that fought during the course of the three English Civil Wars experienced the desertion of soldiers that had not wanted to fight and did not want to leave their local districts.[92]

The contemporary rules of war during the English Civil Wars actually meant that there could be few or no prisoners of war taken once a battle, skirmish, or a siege had ended. That was under the proviso that the winning side could kill all remaining enemy soldiers if the enemy had refused to surrender or accept quarter when it was offered. As will be demonstrated to be on the losing side during the English Civil Wars when a battle, skirmish, or siege were finally over could literally be fatal rather than resulting in being taken prisoners of war for the duration of the conflict.[93] Throughout the course of the first English Civil Wars the contending sides theoretically had the ability to put trial any of the soldiers, sailors, and the commanders of the other side that they had captured. However for the second as well as the third of the English Civil Wars it was the English Parliament in general and the New Model Army in particular that could put on trial any of its opponents, most notably Charles I himself.[94]

Over all the English Civil Wars in military terms were dominated by

---

[92]Dodds, 1995 p. 176

[93]Royale, 2004 p. 1

[94]Hill, 1980 p. 110

the all-conquering New Model Army and its most important commander Oliver Cromwell meaning that together they had a great deal of influence over how prisoners of war were treated. Oliver Cromwell and the New Model Army did not always chose to take prisoners of war in the wake of winning battles, as well as successfully completing sieges. Besides during the English Civil Wars period it was usually left to the discretion of the victorious military commander to decide whether or not quarter was given, or the losers were killed en masse.[95] In other words to chose whether or not their defeated foes died by the sword or became prisoners of war instead. As the rules of war were understood and interpreted during the English Civil Wars once quarter had been refused the victorious commanders could chose to treat their opponents with as much or as little mercy as they wanted. There were different factors that determined whether the victors opted to be merciful or instead to act with the utmost severity once victory had been won. Royalist propaganda always portrayed the king and his military commanders as been more honourable than their opponents yet chivalry was not always evident once battles, skirmishes, and sieges came to an end. There were some vague and informal understandings between all sides that prisoners would not be treated harshly, and would not be punished without a trial or hearing.[96]

---

[95]Poulsen, 1984 p. 78

[96]Kenyon & Ohlmeyer, 1998 p. 201

The three kingdoms of Charles I inadvertently drifted into the first of the English Civil Wars during the course of 1642.[97] The government of Charles I could be blamed for promoting all be it unintentionally the events that led to the outbreak of the first conflict in October 1642 at the inconclusive Battle of Edgehill.[98] It was the decision of Charles I to introduce a modified version of the English Common Book of Prayer into Scottish church services backfired disastrously and led to the Bishops War.[99] The Scots formed their own army, its efficiency improved by the presence of Alexander and David Lesley who had experience of fighting in the Thirty Years War. Events in Scotland soon escalated out of the king's control but he had nobody to blame apart from himself and William Laud, the Archbishop of Canterbury.[100]

Aside from occasional troubles in Ireland there had been no major fighting in the British Isles for a few decades, and the hastily assembled English armies of Charles I proved completely inadequate for fighting the Bishops War.[101] It was probably a failure compounded due to the Protestants within the English armies being unwilling to fight the Scottish Presbyterians when they had similar religious and political beliefs.[102] The expensive failure to defeat the Scots in the Bishops War forced Charles I to reluctantly recall Parliament in order to drive them out of England.[103] After the failure of the Short Parliament, Charles I's relationship with the Puritan

---

[97] Schama, 2001 p. 320

[98] Dodds, 1995 p. 117

[99] Hirst, 1999 p. 157

[100] Chadwick, 1990 p. 239

[101] Brice, 1994 p. 74

[102] Royale, 2004 p. 112

[103] Carlin, 1999 p. 30

elements of the Long Parliament was so acrimonious that it resulted in the first English Civil War.[104] Whilst the king and the Long Parliament disagreed over the raising of taxes and the control of the army there was a major rebellion in Ireland that ended any prospect of a peaceful compromise.[105] The killing of Protestant planters in Ulster would also act as a precursor to massacres, summary executions, and atrocities during the course of the subsequent English Civil Wars.[106] Oliver Cromwell would later justify his actions in 1649 as gaining revenge against "the barbarous and bloodthirsty Irish".[107]

At the start of the English Civil Wars there was no initial thought given to how prisoners of war should be treated, mainly because nobody expected the conflicts to last so long. From a legal as well as a constitutional perspective all those people that fought against Charles I were technically traitors and could expect harsh punishment for their deviance of the royal will.[108] Had Charles I retained full control over his three kingdoms then the political and military leaders as well as the majority of the Scots Presbyterian and English Parliamentary forces could have expected to be executed at worst or imprisoned for very long sentences at best.[109]

The knowledge that the king would almost certainly have the Parliamentary leaders executed for treason arguably increased the resolve of hard-liners such as Oliver Cromwell to carry on fighting.[110] The Royalists claimed that they were more chivalrous than their

---

[104] Poulsen, 1984 p. 78

[105] Schama, 2001 p. 320

[106] Fraser, 1973 p. 76

[107] Abbott, 1937 p. 107

[108] Coffey, 2000 p. 129

[109] Fraser, 1973 p. 87

[110] Carlin, 1999 p. 30

enemies were, but in reality the gentry would play a large role in all the armies involved in fighting the English Civil Wars.[111] As the English Parliamentary forces and their Scottish Presbyterian allies held most of the territories that made it harder for the Royalists to put other prisoners of war on trial.[112] The Royalists were to use military tribunals to convict prisoners of war of treason, as well as resorting to summary executions. Charles I did establish courts in his make shift capital of Oxford, yet these had little influence over Royalist forces.[113] Both sides found it difficult to find adequate accommodation for their captives leading to prisoners being held in churches, and occasionally organised exchanges of prisoners. For instance, prisoners taken at the Battle of Westhougton in December 1642 were exchanged in January 1643. Prisoner exchanges were convenient for all sides, as they got their own soldiers back and were not responsible for looking after so many prisoners of war.[114]

Charles I could demonstrate a great deal of mercy towards his adversaries. After a victory at Lostwithiel the king even released all of the prisoners of war that had been taken, and ordered the punishment of his soldiers that had acted brutally towards their prisoners.[115] As the first English Civil War dragged on, the lack of food and money available to the Royalist forces made them less generous towards their prisoners of war and civilians alike, out of scarcity rather than malice. Even when concerted efforts were made for the good treatment of prisoners of war the reality was that a lack of food, medicines, and basic sanitary provisions put all soldiers, prisoners, and civilians at risk of premature death in the wake of battles and sieges.[116]

---

[111]Kenyon & Ohlmeyer, 1998 p. 201

[112]Dodds, 1995 p. 160

[113]Fraser, 2004 p. 344

[114]www.nationalarchives.gov.uk

[115]Dodds, 1995 p. 159

[116]Schama, 2001 p. 235

The Scots and English Parliamentary sides in theory at least had control of the majority of law courts, yet did not use them to decide how prisoners of war were treated after being captured. Basically the ways in which prisoners of war were treated was down to the discretion of the military commandos upon the ground as well as how disciplined their armies were.[117] The military commanders might decide to allow defeated enemies quarter, yet if they did not fully control their own troops that meant that men were killed, rather than taken prisoner of war. The Battle of Edgehill set the precedent with regard to the taking of prisoners of war during the first English Civil War, few were taken if possible.[118] Both sides would often leave their seriously wounded on the battlefield to die, as they did not have enough medical resources to treat the most gravely injured. Often wounds and infections killed more men than the actual fighting. The ill discipline of the Royalist cavalry at the Battle of Edgehill proved significant, if they had reformed earlier they could have decisively defeated the Parliamentary forces of the Earl of Essex. The cavalry of Prince Rupert when it charged induced panic in the Parliamentary army yet it failed to swiftly return to the battlefield.[119] The Royalist failure to win decisively at Edgehill meant that Charles I was unable to reach London to bring the first English Civil War to a swift conclusion.[120]

The opportunity to take prisoners of war also arose in the minor skirmishes, as well as the major battles. In England the Midlands, the South West region, as well as Yorkshire were regarded as being strategically important leading to skirmishes and sieges.[121] The control of ports such as Bristol, Hull and Scarborough were also highly important for the final outcome of the first English Civil War,

---

[117] Royale, 2004 p. 10

[118] Foard, 2004 p. 31

[119] Bulstrode, 1971 p. 84

[120] Dodds, 1995 p. 118

[121] Fraser, 2004 p. 345

to allow or prevent the import of weapons from abroad.[122] Some of these skirmishes and sieges witnessed atrocities; brutality and a preference for killing defeated foes, rather than taking prisoners of war. Such skirmishes occurred in Birmingham, Bradford, Leeds, Pontefract, and Wakefield. Both sides showed brutality and committed atrocities when it suited their commanders or indeed if their soldiers got carried away in the moment of victory. Both sides also produced propaganda to publicise their own victories, as well as portraying the actions of the other side in as bad light as possible. For instance, when Prince Rupert of the Palatine fought Parliamentary forces in Birmingham during 1643 the Royalist publications hailed it as a victory. On the other hand Prince Rupert was then dubbed the 'Butcher of Birmingham' in Parliamentary accounts and publications.[123] In contrast, when the Royalist forces under Prince Rupert captured the port of Bristol its former Parliamentary defenders were allowed to become prisoners of war peacefully and undisturbed.[124]

The Royalist efforts to lift the Parliamentary siege of York in the summer of 1644 resulted in the largest battle of all the English Civil Wars at Marston Moor, and a disastrous defeat for them.[125] The allied forces were under the command of Alexander Lesley ennobled as the Earl of Levan, and Lord Fairfax who both left the battle early fearing that the Royalists had won.[126] The Royalists appeared to be winning the battle of Marston Moor at one stage until the intervention of Oliver Cromwell, Sir Thomas Fairfax, and David Lesley proved to be decisive. The Parliamentary forces at Marston Moor did take around a thousand prisoners of war. That figure of Royalist men captured would have been considerably higher but for

---

[122] Gardiner & Wenborn, 1995 p. 212

[123] Sherwood, 1997 p. 36

[124] Smith, 1997 p. 235

[125] Fraser, 1973 p. 127

[126] Gardiner & Wenborn, 1995 p. 502

the bulk of the Royalist infantry fighting to the death. It was the White Coats under the command of the Earl of Newcastle that had refused to accept quarter when it was offered, with the Parliamentarian commanders admiring their brave resistance. The loss of the Earl of Newcastle's White Coats was a grave setback for the prospects of the Royalists cause ending successfully. Oliver Cromwell and David Lesley would have spared these brave men, yet were relieved of the burden of providing for them as prisoners of war.[127]

The defeat at Marston Moor did not immediately lead to the collapse of the Royalist war effort; indeed the Royalist forces were able to make gains in the South West, as well as the Midlands.[128] The failure to take full and immediate advantage of the victory at Marston Moor led to the eventual passing of the Self-Denying Ordinance and the emergence of the New Model Army.[129] Before the New Model Army could deal a decisive blow against the Royalist forces under Prince Rupert carried out some of the worst atrocities of the English Civil War. When the Parliamentary garrison at Leicester failed to defend the city, the Royalist soldiers murdered, raped, pillaged, and plundered at will after it fell. No distinction was drawn between the Parliamentary garrison and the civilian population; none of the 200 Scots prisoners of war were allowed to survive, being shot on the same day that they surrendered.[130]

The main turning point of the first English Civil War was the Battle of Naseby, when the New Model Army without the Scottish Presbyterians (who were in Scotland attempting to defeat the Marquis of Montrose) defeated the smaller Royalist forces.[131] Estimates at the time gave the strength of the New Model Army at

---

[127] Gardiner & Wenborn, 1995 p. 167

[128] Royale, 2004 p. 308

[129] Fraser, 1973 p. 142

[130] Sherwood, 1997 p. 39

[131] Schama, 2001 p. 231

Naseby around 15,000 men, a few thousand more than the Royalist army was.[132] This defeat effectively ended any lingering prospects of the Royalists winning the first English Civil War. Whilst the Royalist forces had been able to brutally take Leicester weeks earlier they proved to be no match for the well drilled not to mention well armed New Model Army. Unlike earlier skirmishes and even Marston Moor a rather more substantial number of Royalist soldiers were captured at Naseby and therefore became prisoners of war. Around 4,500 Royalist soldiers were taken as prisoners of war and were then forced to march through the streets of London in a mocking parody of a victory parade. The prisoners of war captured at Naseby aside from been publicly mocked in London were not particularly well treated. A majority of the Royalist soldiers captured during the battle were Welsh infantry regiments, some of whom had their wives attached to their army's pay train, worse was to befall these women during the battle at Naseby.[133]

Some New Model Army soldiers were responsible for the killing of dozens of women attached to the Royalist pay train during the course of the battle at Naseby. Those soldiers thought to be actually responsible for the killing of these women were unpunished, despite Parliamentary publications admitting that unarmed women had been killed during the battle. The misbehaviour of the New Model Army was excused in the Parliamentary publications as the slaughtered women were alleged to have been prostitutes or Irish Catholics, reflecting the religious extremism of some of the Parliamentarian soldiers and its leaders.[134] In late 1644 the Long Parliament passed an ordinance that required that its forces immediately execute any Irish Catholics that they captured amongst Royalist prisoners of war.[135] It appears that under the auspices of this discriminatory ordinance that only thirteen Irish Catholic prisoners were unlucky enough to be

---

[132] Mercurius Civicus, 12th-18th June 1645, quoted in Foard

[133] Royale, 2004 p. 341

[134] Dodds, 1995 p. 176

[135] Hirst, 1999 p. 225

summarily executed. After Prince Rupert retaliated by hanging thirteen randomly selected Parliamentary prisoners of war the ordinance was then ignored by the officers and men of the New Model Army.[136]

As the first English Civil War slowly reached its conclusion the New Model Army and the Scottish Presbyterians had to go around England, Scotland, and Wales taking the remaining Royalist strongholds one by one increasing the number of prisoners of war in their custody. Briefly the Marquis of Montrose had seemed to over the Royalists' hope of overthrowing the Presbyterian domination of Scotland. The Marquis of Montrose and the Scottish Presbyterians that eventually defeated showed no mercy towards each other and neither side bothered to take any prisoners of war.[137]

By the end of the first English Civil War there were serious divisions within the Long Parliament and also between the English Parliamentarians and the Scottish Presbyterians. In the Long Parliament its Presbyterian faction had been inclined to reach a settlement with Charles I and they also happened to be afraid of the power of the New Model Army in general and of Oliver Cromwell in particular.[138] The English Presbyterian faction therefore attempted to demobilise the New Model Army was the fighting had finally finished. The leadership of the New Model Army refused to allow its regiments to be disbanded at least until after the fate of the king had been decided. Charles I believed that the falling out amongst his opponents gave him the opportunity to regain what he had lost during the first English Civil War with the help of the more moderate elements amongst his enemies.[139] Sir Thomas Fairfax for one was aware that Charles I was attempting to take advantage of his position as "the Golden Ball cast between the two parties".[140]

---

[136]Kenyon & Ohlmeyer, 1998 p. 112

[137]Royale, 2004 p. 342

[138]Gardiner & Wenborn, 1995 p. 546

[139]Fraser, 1973 p. 192

The uncertain future of the New Model Army was not a good thing for the Royalist prisoners of war held in custody. After all with the bulk of the New Model Army remaining unpaid and lacking resources for themselves at this point regarded the good treatment of prisoners of war as being a burden that it could not afford.[141] The leadership of the New Model Army by the time that the first English Civil War finished was disillusioned with the Presbyterians within the English Parliament as well as no longer trusting their Scottish Presbyterian allies, and decided to take action to prevent them from dealing with the king.[142] By 1647 the New Model Army held a political trump card that could not be bettered, for it had gained control of the one prisoner of war that its leadership wanted to punish the most, Charles I himself.[143]

---

[140]Fairfax, 1837 p. 112

[141]Royale, 2004 p. 340

[142]Fraser, 1973 p. 193

[143]Hill, 1980 p. 106

The way in which the civil war affected the Guilds of Chester

Outlined below is a discussion of the way or ways in which the civil war affected the Guilds of Chester. Furthermore this discussion will go on to evaluate why as well as how the civil war was able to affect the Guilds of Chester besides exploring whether or not other Guilds had similar experiences during that traumatic period. The following discussion will also explore the short - term and the long - term affect of the English Civil Wars upon the Guilds of Chester. In many respects the assumption that the civil war given its associated social and economic consequences is an understandable one to reach, whether or not it is justified by any degree of evidence or well - established facts. Certainly as will be discussed the English Civil Wars were arguably the predominant catalyst as well as consequence of major economic, social, and political, not to mention demographic changes throughout Britain and Ireland taken as a whole. How such changes impacted and the degree of influence upon the city of Chester and its Guilds in particular is the main focus of this short evaluation.

The Guilds of Chester were arguably at the start of the English Civil Wars in 1642 at least a highly important component of the social and economic structures within Chester and the local area surrounding it. The Guilds of Chester were at the beginning of the 1640s organisations whose members included the wealthiest and the most influential men (women were of course excluded) inside the city limits of Chester itself.[144] That the Guilds of Chester were regarded as being important was not particularly surprising at that point in time. After all the Guilds had been a bastion of artisan and skilled workers privileges right across the country despite their importance already been in gradual decline.[145] Despite that gradual decline it

---

[144]Hill, 1980 p.22

[145]Morgan, 1993 p. 367

would not have been too unreasonable in 1642 to assume that the Guilds of Chester would remain at the hub of their local surrounding area, as they had been since the Middle Ages.[146] At the start of the 1640s Chester had a dozen or more Guilds related to the various crafts, industries, and trades within the city. For example there were guilds for brewers, drapers, metal workers, furniture makers, tailors, as well as merchants.[147]

The Guilds of Chester had been central to the local administration of the city as well as its organisation; it's apprentices and the majority of its tradesmen.[148] The Guilds of Chester had survived the drastic culling of such religiously based organisations during the reigns of Henry VIII and Edward VI.[149] To a large extent the Guilds of Chester had survived if not thrived until the outbreak of the civil war because they deemed to be useful organisations economically, socially, and also politically.[150] Guilds were organisations, which tended to defend the privileged positions of their membership and apprentices from workers that were not members of these bodies.[151] Guilds were not as strong in areas that already started to industrialise like Birmingham, Coventry, and London. Places with weak guilds were politically more radical. Chester with its powerful guilds was strongly Royalist.[152]

---

[146] Gardiner & Wenborn, 1995 p. 154

[147] Past Uncovered: Quarterly Newsletter of Chester Arch. Autumn 1998.From: 'Early modern Chester 1550-1762: Economy and society, 1550-1642', A History of the County of Chester: Volume 5 part 1: The City of Chester: General History and Topography (2003), pp. 102-109. URL: http://www.british-history.ac.uk/report.aspx?compid=19195 Date accessed: 10 February 2009.

[148] Hill, 1980 p. 33

[149] Schama, 2001 p. 324

[150] Gardiner & Wenborn, 1995 p. 154

[151] MacCulloch, 2004 p. 400

[152] Hill, 1980 p. 22

Indeed it was the capacity of the guilds to organise and mobilise economic, manual, and military resources that made them useful for Parliament as well as for the Royalists. Throughout England the majority of guilds assisted the rival sides either through enthusiasm or because they were forced to do so.[153] For example the guilds of Coventry and London were strongly inclined towards supporting the Parliamentary forces in contrast to those of Chester that were overwhelmingly Royalist in their sympathies. The Guilds of Chester would eventually suffer for their loyalty towards Charles I due to Parliament winning the civil war.[154]

Neither the Parliamentarians nor the Royalists were against the guilds in general or the Guilds of Chester in particular. The way in which the civil war was mostly linked to the high human, economic, and social costs linked with that conflict. Both sides needed bullion, weapons, and money, as well as soldiers.[155] The members of the Guilds of Chester just like the bulk of their contemporaries experienced large - scale depletion, or at least use of their resources during the course of the civil war.[156] The city of Chester began as previously mentioned the civil war on the Royalist side with the resources and the manpower of the Chester based guilds being used by the King.[157]

Over the long - term the failure of the Royalists to capture London after the Battle of Edgehill meant that the civil war lasted longer. A longer war thus had a far more detrimental affect upon the Guilds of Chester whilst they controlled much of Cheshire and Lancashire whose populations were generally sympathetic towards the King's

---

[153] Hill, 1980 p. 22

[154] Schama, 2001 p.324

[155] Dodds, 1996 p. 169

[156] Coward, 1980 p. 141

[157] Hill, 1990 p. 22

cause.[158] However within the first year or so of the civil war it became apparent that the Northern areas of England including Chester that the Royalists controlled could not match the resources that the Parliamentary forces were able to obtain and subsequently use.[159] In their desperate position the Royalists had to make an even greater use of the Guilds of Chester's dwindling men and materials.[160] In 1643 The Guilds contributed to the raising of £500 in order to upgrade the defences of Chester's city walls.[161] In July the council of Chester agreed to contribute £600 and more troops for the Royalist cause after the defeat at Marston Moor.[162]

It is not surprising that the Guilds of Chester were adversely affected by the Royalist defeat in the civil war, although a Royalist victory could probably have proved to be similarly expensive for the citizens of Chester and the members of their Guilds.[163] The Parliamentarians who heavily taxed the areas that they controlled for the entire civil war period were inclined to tax former areas such as Chester punitively. The Guild members within Chester were aware that Parliament had no qualms in taxing them or making them serve in the New Model Army for the duration of the civil war. The lands and estates of the richest Royalists including the members of the Chester Guilds were liable to be confiscated.[164]

---

[158] Ashley, 1990 p. 10

[159] Bennett, 1986 p. 20

[160] Hill, 1990 p. 22

[161] www.british-history.ac.uk/report.aspx?compid=19198

[162] Morris, Siege of Chester, 45-9, 55-7From: 'Early modern Chester 1550-1762: The civil war and interregnum, 1642-60', A History of the County of Chester: Volume 5 part 1: The City of Chester: General History and Topography (2003), pp. 115-125. URL: http://www.british-history.ac.uk/report.aspx?compid=19198 Date accessed: 10 February 2009.

[163] Bennett, 1995 p. 38

[164] Bennett, 1995 p. 67

The cost of supporting the Royalist war effort alongside the confiscation, levies, and taxes to Parliament placed a considerable strain on the members of the Guilds within Chester. Eventually Parliament became adept at raising the men, money, and supplies needed to make the New Model Army the most effective fighting force during the course of the civil war.[165] The Parliamentary administration raised money and equipped the New Model Army without any long - term regard to the economic dislocation that was caused especially in former Royalist strongholds such as Chester. Victory was more important than worrying about what happened to guilds across the length and breadth of England certainly in the opinion of Parliamentary hard-liners like Oliver Cromwell.[166]

The affect that the civil war had upon the Guilds of Chester was increased due to the long - running Parliamentary siege of the city itself.[167] The Royalists were initially successful in being able to overcome the population of Chester's desire to remain neutral throughout the conflict. The Guild members alongside non-members could understand the benefits of remaining neutral.[168]

However the Royalists had quickly asserted their authority and then put the city the king's side. Chester was deemed to be strategically important by both sides because it was a port with access to the Irish Sea.[169] For as long as the Royalists held Chester there was the potential for them to bring arms, soldiers, and supplies from Ireland in order to overcome the greater resources of the Parliamentarians.[170] For the Parliamentarians the taking of Chester and its port was an

---

[165] Bennett, 1995 p. 38

[166] Hill, 1990 p. 108

[167] Fraser, 1973 p.280

[168] Fraser, 1973 p.280

[169] Hutton, 1981 p. 2

[170] Hutton, 1981 p. 2

important stepping stone on the path to winning the civil war. It was not a priority target like other cities and towns which is why enough forces were not enough forces gathered to take Chester until February 1646.[171]

The siege of Chester had curtailed the food and the other supplies coming into the city whilst conversely its Royalist garrison used up the resources of the Guilds within the city walls.[172] After the New Model Army took control of Chester in February 1646 the city did not have to endure another siege or nearby military engagements.[173] The Parliamentarians as previously noted made sure that the Guilds and other people within Chester actually contributed fully to the new regime as well as the New Model Army.[174] Briefly in 1648 Scottish Royalist army threatened to bring renewed fighting in the vicinity of Chester. Further disruptions were prevented by the crushing victory of the New Model Army at the Battle of Preston.[175]

Over all it is not surprising that the way in which the civil war had a detrimental affect upon the Guilds of Chester. Guild members across the country had frequently fought in the civil war whether voluntarily or being press-ganged into the rival armies whilst that who had not experienced military service had paid higher taxes and levies.[176] The civil war had seriously interrupted both domestic and foreign trade, which was certainly a disadvantage for ports like Chester.[177] The Guilds of Chester did not find that there any financial benefits of the fighting in England finishing. Whilst individual

---

[171] Schama, 2001 p. 323

[172] Morrell, 1990 p. 59

[173] Barnard, 1982 p. 120

[174] Bennett, 1995 p. 97

[175] Dodds, 1996 p. 172

[176] Hill, 1990 p. 22

[177] Gardiner & Wenborn, 1995 p. 154

traders might have made money form supplying the needs of the New Model Army units sent to Ireland the city as a whole had the high costs of housing such troops before they set sail to Ireland.[178]

Not only was trade disrupted, agricultural production was also reduced due to farmers and farm workers having to perform military service instead of attending to their crops and their livestock.[179] Royalist and Parliamentary armies took a large share of food and other supplies from the villages, towns, and cities they passed through, although the New Model Army often paid for whatever they consumed. Generally the New Model Army did not carry out mass murder, pillage, and rape when they captured towns and cities. The citizens and the Guilds of Chester were treated with considerably less brutality than their counterparts in towns captured by the Royalists.[180]

In conclusion the way in which the civil war affected the main Guilds of Chester were adversely so. The Guilds of Chester were markedly pro – Royalist at the start of the civil war mainly due to the assumption that a victory for the king would best serve their social and economic interests. Chester as noted above was deemed to be strategically important by both sides because it was a port with access to the Irish Sea. The heavy cost of supporting the ultimately doomed Royalist war effort alongside the confiscation, levies, and taxes to Parliament placed a considerable strain on the members of the Guilds within Chester. The Parliamentary victory in the civil war was probably the main cause for that conflict having a detrimental impact upon the Guilds of Chester.

---

[178] Past Uncovered: Quarterly Newsletter of Chester Arch. Autumn 1998.From: 'Early modern Chester 1550-1762: Economy and society, 1550-1642', A History of the County of Chester: Volume 5 part 1: The City of Chester: General History and Topography (2003), pp. 102-109. URL: http://www.british-history.ac.uk/report.aspx?compid=19195 Date accessed: 10 February 2009.

[179] Bennett, 1995 p. 38

[180] Hill, 1990 p. 107

Bibliography

Ashley, M. *The English Civil War* (1990) 2nd edition, Alan Sutton Publishing
Barnard, T The English Republic (1982) Longman
Bennett, M Contribution, and Assessment: Financial Exactions in the English Civil War (1986) War and Society
Bennett, M The English Civil War, (1995) Longman
Coward, B The Stuart Age, (1980) Longman
Dodds, G. L. Battles in Britain 1066 – 1746 (1996) Brockhampton Press
Fraser, A. *Cromwell Our Chief of Men* (1973) Weidenfeld & Nicholson.
Gardiner & Wenborn (1995) the History Today Companion to British History, Collins and Brown Ltd, London
Hutton, R The Structure of the Royalist Party 1642 – 1646 (1981) Historical Journal
Hill C. *the Century of Revolution 1603 – 1714* 2nd edition (1980) Routledge.
MacCulloch D, Reformation – Europe's House Divided (2004) Penguin Books, London
Morgan K.O (editor) *The Oxford Popular History of Britain (1993)* Paragon.
Morrill, J. Oliver Cromwell and the English Revolution (1990) Longman
Morris, Siege of Chester, 45-9, 55-7 From: 'Early modern Chester 1550-1762: The civil war and interregnum, 1642-60', A History of the County of Chester: Volume 5 part 1: The City of Chester: General History and Topography (2003), pp. 115-125. URL: http://www.british-history.ac.uk/report.aspx?compid=19198 Date accessed: 10 February 2009.
Schama, S. *A History of Britain – The British Wars 1603-1776 (2001),* BBC Worldwide, London.
www.british-history.ac.uk/report.aspx?compid=19198

Chapter Two – the treatment of prisoners of war during the second and third English Civil Wars

Although the New Model Army won the first English Civil War the divisions within the Long Parliament and the falling out with the Scottish Presbyterians led to the outbreak of the second English Civil War, mainly to determine the fate of Charles I.[181]
The outbreak of the second English Civil War would eventually greatly strengthen the military and also the political power of the New Model Army, which would be detrimental to all its enemies. On the other hand for the remaining prisoners of war in its custody if it gained greater amounts of supplies their treatment might eventually improve.[182] At this point both the English Presbyterians inside the Long Parliament and the Scottish Presbyterians wanted to maintain the monarchy after forcing concessions from Charles I. The king himself managed to escape to Scotland, and then hoped that the subsequent second English Civil War would allow to regain his former dominant political position and eclipse the might of the New Model Army.[183]

The Royalists planned to launch simultaneous uprisings throughout England and Wales to coincide with an invasion by the Scottish Presbyterians from north of the border.[184] The leadership of the New Model Army especially Oliver Cromwell and Henry Ireton were determined to quickly crush their Royalist, English and Scottish Presbyterian opponents. The determination of the New Model Army to destroy all opposition meant that it was reluctant to take prisoners of war or offer any quarter at all during battle and sieges.[185] All of the uprisings in England and Wales were ruthlessly put down with scant regard for the fair treatment of prisoners of war. The Royalist

---

[181]Schama, 2001 p. 233

[182]Smith, 1991 p. 9

[183]Dodds, 1995 p. 175

[184]Fraser, 2004 p. 347

[185]Smith, 1997 p. 234

uprisings in England and Wales were also more of an annoyance than a serious threat to the military supremacy of the New Model Army, no real test for Oliver Cromwell and Sir Thomas Fairfax. The Scottish Presbyterian forces that invaded England in the second English Civil War were not the veteran armies of the Bishops War and the first English Civil War, which proved fatal to their chances of beating the New Model Army.[186]

The new Scottish Presbyterian forces were instead inadequately trained raw recruits. The gravely inexperienced Scottish Presbyterian forces actually got as far as Preston when their luck and that of Charles I ran out. The New Model Army swiftly won the very one-sided battle at Preston, resulting in the recapture of the most important prisoner of war of all, Charles I. The victory at Preston ended the second English Civil War and resulted in the decision of the Rump Parliament in conjunction with the New Model Army to put the king on trial. The New Model Army demonstrated its ruthlessness during the second English Civil War and it hoped that the execution of Charles I would put an end to the fighting in the British Isles once and for all.[187]

To make the trial of Charles I increasingly likely the Long Parliament was cleansed of Presbyterian members via Pride's Purge. Pride himself argued that the king should be imprisoned, as "no further security" would be unavailable until that happened.[188]

The trial and the execution of Charles I did not however bring peace or even stability to his former three kingdoms.[189] Even members of the Rump Parliament were unsure about putting the king on trial; the Earl of Northumberland saying it was "very unreasonable".[190] Instead his death as a martyr for the Royal and the church of

---

[186]Gardiner & Wenborn, 1995 p. 168

[187]Royale, 2004 p. 476

[188]Mercurius Pragmaticus, 2 October 1648, quoted in Foard

[189]Royale, 2004 p. 490

[190]Mercurius Pragmaticus, 3 January 1649, quoted in Foard

England causes was mainly responsible for starting the third and final English Civil War. The renewal of fighting was due to the Irish and the Scottish as much as the English Royalists refusing to accept the abolition of the monarchy and support for making the Prince of Wales the next king. Due to the gravity of the situation the Rump Parliament decided to send Oliver Cromwell and the strongest regiments of the New Model Army over to Ireland to establish it's authority there. Oliver Cromwell went as the new head of the New Model Army as Sir Thomas Fairfax refused to go to Ireland. The Irish Royalists held strong positions and were ably led by the Earl of Ormand who had also managed to get Roman Catholics and Protestants to co-exist in his army.[191]

The problem for the Earl of Ormand was that Oliver Cromwell and the majority of the New Model Army hated the Irish and also wanted to avenge the Ulster massacres of 1641.[192] No distinction was made between the Protestants and the Roman Catholics within the Earl of Ormand's forces, Cromwell intending to ruthlessly assert English Parliamentary control over all of Ireland. The first target for the New Model Army was Drogheda, which had the Irish garrison refused to accept the offer of quarter from the New Model Army.[193] Cromwell decided that nobody in Drogheda should be allowed to survive once his soldiers got inside that town. Cromwell was well aware that his decision would entail the deaths of thousands of soldiers and civilians yet justified it by claiming it would shorten the war in Ireland. The contemporary rules of war would have deemed the actions of the New Model Army once Drogheda fell as being legally acceptable. Oliver Cromwell had to leave Ireland before it had been fully subjugated placing his son-in-law Henry Ireton in charge. The New Model Army had not taken any prisoners of war instead killing all its opponents once the offer of quarter had been refused. The next target for the New Model Army was the town of Wexford, which was duly taken after a brief siege. As quarter had

---

[191] Royale, 2004 p. 521

[192] Fraser, 1973 p. 331

[193] Royale, 2004 p. 522

been refused none was given when the siege ended brutally.[194]

Oliver Cromwell had been recalled from Ireland by the Rump Parliament in order to deal with the revival of the Royalist threat from Scotland.[195] The Scottish Presbyterians had crowned Charles II and intended to restore the monarchy in all three kingdoms. Unlike the second English Civil War the Scottish Presbyterian forces contained the veterans of the Bishops War and the first English Civil War. Therefore, the Scottish Presbyterian forces posed a greater threat to the Rump Parliament. Oliver Cromwell was able to outwit his former ally David Leslie at the Battle of Dunbar in September 1650. The New Model Army attacked at night and thus inflicted thousands of fatalities at a minimal cost to itself and whilst not bothering to take any prisoners of war, Cromwell showed his tactical astuteness by allowing the Scottish Presbyterian forces to invade England with his regiments following behind them. The further south the Scottish Presbyterian forces went the weaker they became, with Cromwell biding his time to their rear.

A year to the day after Dunbar the Scottish Presbyterians marched into the trap set for them at Worcester, their army was much less experienced due to the losses inflicted upon them at Dunbar and Charles II officers that he did not like due to their more extreme religious beliefs. The Scottish Presbyterian forces weakened by its march down to Worcester fought bravely until they surrendered having the good sense to accept quarter when it was offered to them. For Cromwell the stunning victory at Worcester was only marred by the successful escape of Charles II form the battlefield? Thousands of Scottish Presbyterians were captured their treatment as prisoners of war not been as bad as it would have been in the first English Civil War. The victory of the New Model Army at Worcester marked the end of the English Civil War with Charles II opting to stay in exile and waiting for the death of Cromwell. That in the end was the most - sound strategy of all as it avoided further crushing defeats and stopped any more Royalists needlessly becoming

---

[194]Schama, 2001 p. 236

[195]Hill, 1980 p. 106

prisoners of war. Whilst Cromwell had been the master of every battlefield with the New Model Army he was unable to find a viable long-term alternative to the monarchy.[196]

During the second and third English Civil War the military superiority of the New Model Army was blatantly obvious both to its commanders and the opponents attempting to defeat it. Hand in hand with the fighting qualities of the New Model Army went the ruthless leadership of Oliver Cromwell who was determined that the Royalists should be defeated once and for all. Cromwell always defended the interests of the New Model Army, as it was his most important political weapon, as well as being such a potent military force. During the second and third English Civil Wars the New Model Army was the only force that had the capacity to take a large number of prisoners of war and possibly treat them well by the standards of the day. In contrast the Royalists, the Irish and the Scottish Presbyterians lacked the resources to accommodate a small number of prisoners of war let alone successfully overcome the military might of the New Model Army. Divisions within the New Model Army itself could have been more threatening to the Rump Parliament, with Cromwell personally having to crush mutinies and dealt with the Levellers. In truth the New Model Army could pick and choose when to take prisoners of war and how to subsequently treat them. The Scottish Presbyterians had been former allies, yet that did not meant that they received preferential treatment as prisoners of war than any of the other enemies of the New Model Army.[197]

---

[196] Schama, 2001 p. 238

[197] Smith, 1997 p. 325

Conclusions

Therefore during the English Civil Wars between 1642 and 1651 prisoners of war were not generally treated well, especially by modern standards. The poor treatment of prisoners of war was partly caused by a lack of resources to look after them properly and sometimes a desire to make them suffer for fighting on the losing side. How well prisoners of war were actually treated was largely dependent upon who was captured and by whom they were captured. None of the military commanders in the English Civil Wars had to take prisoners of war if they had offered quarter and it had been refused. In many ways it was the ordinary soldiers that stood the greatest chance of being fairly or leniently treated as prisoners of war during the English Civil Wars. The Royalist propaganda certainly tried to portray their commanders as being more likely to take prisoners of war and subsequently treat them well than any of their opponents. Officers sometimes faced summary execution after being captured, as they were held responsible for the past actions of their own forces.

The New Model Army proved to be particularly brutal when it suited them, for instance, in Ireland especially at Drogheda and Wexford in 1649. The Earl of Newcastle's White Coats had been cut down at Marston Moor as they had refused to surrender, whilst a thousand or so Royalists did become prisoners of war as a result of being defeated at Marston Moor. There were examples of surrendered soldiers being treated well as prisoners of war such as the Parliamentary garrison of Bristol after its capture by the forces of Prince Rupert. There were also atrocities such as the sack of Leicester by Prince Rupert's army as well as the capture of Drogheda and Wexford by the New Model Army. Such events did not usually lead to the capture of prisoners of war at all. On balance the Royalists seemed more likely to treat prisoners of war well yet that was not guaranteed. The stunning victory of the New Model Army at Naseby led to the capture of thousands of Royalist prisoners of war that were publicly humiliated in London. Some of the Royalist prisoners of war from Naseby had wives that were killed when New Model Army soldiers had killed the women attached to the Royalist pay train.

Bibliography

Abbott W C, Writings and Speeches Of Oliver Cromwell (1937) Cambridge, Massachusetts

Ashley, M. *The English Civil War* (1990) 2nd edition, Alan Sutton Publishing

Brice, K. Access to History- The Early Stuarts 1603-1640 (1994) Hodder & Stoughton, London

Bulstrode R, Memoirs (1971)

Carlin, N. Historical Association Studies - *The Causes of the English Civil War* (1999) Blackwell Publishers Ltd, Oxford.

Chadwick, O. *The Penguin History of the Church 3 The Reformation,* reprinted (1990) Penguin Books London

Coffey, J. *Persecution and Toleration in Protestant England 1558-1689* - Studies in Modern History (2000), Pearson Education Ltd, Harlow

Dodds, G. L. Battles in Britain 1066 – 1746 (1996) Brockhampton Press

Fairfax T, Memoirs (1837)

Foard G, Naseby – the decisive campaign (2004) Pen & Sword Military, Barnsley

Fraser, A. *Cromwell Our Chief of Men* (1973) Weidenfeld & Nicholson, London

Fraser R, A people's History of Britain, (20040 Pimlico, London

Gardiner & Wenborn *The History Today Companion to British History (1995)* Collins and Brown Ltd, London

Hirst D, England in Conflict 1603 – 1660 (1999) Arnold, London

Kenyon J & Ohlmeyer J, The Civil War – A Military History of England, Scotland, and Ireland (1998), Oxford University Press, Oxford

MacCulloch D, Reformation – Europe's House Divided (2004) Penguin Books, London

Mercurius Civicus, 12th-18th June 1645, quoted in Foard

Mercurius Pragmaticus, 2 October 1648, quoted in Foard

Mercurius Pragmaticus, 3 January 1649, quoted in Foard

Poulsen, C. *the English rebels* (1984) The Journeyman Press,

London & New York

Royale T, Civil War – The Wars of the Three kingdoms 1638 – 1660 (2004) Abacus, London

Schama, S. *A History of Britain - The British Wars 1603-1776 (2001),* BBC Worldwide, London

Sherwood R, The Civil War in the Midlands (1997) Stroud

Smith, D.L, *Oliver Cromwell – Politics and Religion in the English Revolution, 1640 – 1658* (1991) Cambridge University Press

Smith, A G R *the Emergence of a Nation State the Commonwealth of England 1529-1660* (1997) 2nd edition Longman, London and New York

www.nationalarchives.gov.uk

Section 5

Hobbes & Locke – the State of Nature

The evaluations and discussions outlined below are intended to examine the differences John Locke and Thomas Hobbes's notions of the state of nature. These evaluations and discussions will frequently refer to the views expressed by Locke and Hobbes in the Second Treatise of Government, and the Leviathan respectively. The ideas or notions put forward by Locke and Hobbes were, as will be discussed heavily influenced by the events that occurred during their respective lifetimes. The differences between Locke and Hobbes's notions of the state of nature could have arguably caused by their different outlooks, education, and also by their differing personalities. Their differences concerning the notions of the state of nature will be explained by examining the differing objectives behind the writing of the Second Treatise of Government and the Leviathan. Both books would prove to be highly influential works for the development of conservative and liberal political ideologies respectively. The ideological differences in the understanding and presentation of the notions of the state of nature proved very important to the ideological and political contents of these two books. In many ways the works of Locke and Hobbes were the products of the turbulent times in 17th century Britain that culminated in the English Civil Wars and the Glorious Revolution, yet the influence of Locke and Hobbes has carried on through to modern times.

The differences between Locke and Hobbes's understanding and development of the notions of the state of nature started with differing personalities. Thomas Hobbes was a man that favoured political stability, and a strong state to ensure that society did not disintegrate into anarchy or chaos. Hobbes wanted social and political order to be maintained; therefore the onus for all people had to accept the authority of their political, social, and religious superiors. Ultimately all power should reside with the secular government to maintain order and justice. Thus for Hobbes had to exist to keep peoples behaviour under control as they are naturally prone towards social and political disorder, chaos, and potentially

violence.[198] Hobbes view of humanity as presented in the Leviathan was essentially negative, as he was pessimistic about people's behaviour and their basic motivations. He describes the state of nature's affects on human life as making it 'solitary, poor, nasty, brutish and short'.[199] Left to their own devices, people are naturally selfish, and would therefore only look after their own interests, and they would not worry about the morality or the ethical implications of the methods they utilise to serve those interests. People want to put their material needs ahead of everybody else needs.[200] Without political, civic, or religious authorities or institutions the most negative aspects of human behaviour will become apparent, and to the fore. In the absence of any restraining authority, laws, or morality it will be the physically strongest, or mentally most alert and devious that will tend to compete with each other to dominate their societies whether they are developed or primitive. Hobbes's negative perception of human nature and behaviour in turn meant that his notions of the state of nature were correspondingly more likely to be negative in their context and content.[201] Hobbes thought that disobeying governments would lead to a return to the state of nature. Or as he asked in the Leviathan:
'How could a state be governed ... if every individual remained free to obey or not to obey the law according to his private opinion?'[202]

In contrast, John Locke's view of human nature and behaviour was definitely more positive in outlook than Hobbes was. Unlike Hobbes, Locke assumed that if left to their devices would eventually achieve stability, peace, and perhaps even prosperity. Locke was to all intents and purposes an optimist when it came down to what people could achieve prior to authorities or institutions were

---

[198] Eatwell & Wright, 2003 p.72

[199] Heywood, 2003 p. 40

[200] Eatwell & Wright, 2003 p. 108

[201] Eatwell & Wright, 2003 p. 72

[202] Comfort, 1993 p. 343

established. In fact Locke believed that people should still be able to influence or in extreme cases replace their governments.[203] From Locke's perspective people tended towards stability rather than acting in ways that would lead to chaos or anarchy if left unchecked by civic authorities and their associated-armed force and policing powers. Taken as a whole people were more likely to co-operate with each other, at a basic level that co-operation was an essential element of their combined chances of surviving, developing, and eventually prospering as societies and nations. Co-operation allows people to gain food, and accommodation with less effort and less conflict or argument than, when people are competing against each other for everything they need. For the most part people can acquire what they need through co-operating with each other and once barter or monetary systems have been established then that was the time when that level of co-operation and development should increase in that society. Locke does not argue that violence or conflict is not a part of human behaviour, it is not the most logical or inevitable outcome of people living in the state of nature. Rather the structure of civic, political, and religious authorities are able to evolve or emerge as a consequence of people being inclined towards order and co-operation. Co-operation was carried out, as it was logically that it was the most rational way that people could achieve stability and make progress Heywood.[204] Further more unlike Hobbes, Locke believed that the state of nature was something to be learn from, or perhaps even to respect, rather than something to be avoided at all possible cost.[205]

Arguably the ways in which Locke and Hobbes viewed or developed their personal notions of the state of nature were strongly influenced by their own life experiences. It is certainly no coincidence that Hobbes would develop a pessimistic and rather negative set of notions relating to the state of nature, as the events he witnessed were without much doubt more traumatic than those experienced by

---

[203] Heywood, 2000 p.29

[204] Heywood 2003 p. 78

[205] Heywood, 2003 p. 78

Locke.[206] Hobbes was around to witness the disintegration of the Tudor constitutional arrangements, a decline that was accelerated by the monarchy's perennial lack of revenue, intensifying religious divisions, and the extra strains that resulted from having the a monarchy that ruled the three kingdoms of England, Scotland, Ireland (Royale, 2004 p.11). In England, James I and Charles I found it impossible to maintain the traditionally sound relationships between the monarchy, Parliament, and the gentry class from which the majority of MPs, magistrates, and taxpayers came from. Both kings did themselves no favours by clinging on the concept of the divine right of kings.[207] James I had been able to prevent those relationships breaking down completely, whilst Charles I pursued policies that inadvertently did much to cause the subsequent civil wars.[208]

Thomas Hobbes by education, training, and profession had originally been a mathematician. In many respects he was not a man that would be expected to produce a book such as the Leviathan that dealt with political notions such as the state of nature, the legitimacy of governments, and what those governments could or should do to maintain social and political order. Undoubtedly if he had lived in politically and religiously less turbulent times he would have remained a mathematician, and a well paid tutor for the nobility and the gentry. Instead the build up to and the outbreak of the English Civil War would turn Hobbes's considerable intellectual capabilities toward the study of politics, and how it affected society.[209] By inclination Hobbes was originally a loyal supporter of the Stuart cause, believing that the monarchy as the legitimate source of authority, and as the guardian of law and order. His loyalty to the Stuarts was reinforced by his strong links with the Cavendish family, which included the Earl of Newcastle, one of Charles I's loyalist

---

[206] Royale, 2004 p. 251

[207] Royale, 2004 p. 14

[208] Vale, 2006 p. 47

[209] Crystal, 1998 p. 451

supporters and one of the richest as well. The Earl of Newcastle would spend a fortune for the Stuart cause yet went into exile after the defeat at Marston Moor.[210] For Hobbes the outbreak of the English Civil War amply demonstrated the catastrophic political, social, and military consequences of the main civic or political authority collapsing, a collapse that led to violence, disorder, and civil war.[211] The already strong links of Hobbes to the royalist cause were increased by his appointment as the tutor of the future Charles II. The young Prince of Wales was sent into exile to ensure that all would not lost for the Stuarts if Charles I should lose the civil war. Hobbes joined his new pupil into going into exile. It was whilst in exile that Hobbes wrote the Leviathan, as a means to communicate his most forceful thoughts on politics, and philosophy. Hobbes had the good sense to word the Leviathan in such a way that the Commonwealth regime allowed him to return to England from exile.[212]

On the other hand, John Locke who was born later than Hobbes had different life experiences that help to explain their differing notions of the state of nature. Locke had very little experience of life before the English Civil War, and had not witnessed the descent into civil war that had resulted from the breakdown of the political, social, and religious order in England and Scotland. England's declining political authority had resulted in a collapse of control in Ireland, which had been one of Charles I's few successes. Parliament won the English Civil Wars yet at the cost of establishing a governing regime that had more repressive powers than the Stuart monarchy had held previously, and in Oliver Cromwell had a man that had no problem with doing just that. Whilst the Commonwealth regime had such powers, it had also unintentionally helped to strengthen the notions around constitutional government, and the toleration of some political and religious beliefs not associated with the regime itself. However the Commonwealth lacked legitimacy and after Oliver Cromwell's death the only option had been to restore the monarchy

---

[210]Royale, 2004 p. 251

[211]Heywood, 2003 p. 29

[212]Crystal, 1998 p. 451

to avoid further chaos and civil war.[213] Locke came to national prominence during the latter part of Charles II's reign when he was involved in the unsuccessful attempts to bar the Roman Catholic James, Duke of York ascending to the throne. Although the monarchy was supposed to have constitutionally weakened after the Restoration, a shrewd monarch such as Charles II could still yield considerable amounts of power.[214] Locke believed that people only had the duty to obey their government as long as it represented and promoted their best interests, if not the people should be able to find or start a new government that does act to achieve their best interests. Locke wrote the Second Treatise on Government as a retrospective justification or apology for William of Orange gaining the throne via the Glorious Revolution of 1688. As a result of that revolution a constitutional monarchy emerged. The fact that Locke wrote the Second Treatise of Government to justify the Glorious Revolution explains the different emphasis that Locke put on the notions of the state of nature in comparison to Hobbes. Hobbes had tried to dissuade rebellion; Locke was attempting to justify it as a valid political act against tyranny.[215] Or as Heywood states about Locke's arguments 'citizens do not have an absolute obligation to obey laws or accept any form of government'.[216]

Hobbes presents the state of nature as a notion that should only be used to demonstrate the need for all people to obey their governments no matter how tyrannical or authoritarian those regimes might appear to be. All the notions of the state of nature put forward in the Leviathan were bad, as people were incapable of developing and maintaining stable, peaceful, and organised societies without the guiding auspices of a government to direct events. However governments need to be strong, and vigilant to ensure that people always did as they were told. Weak government is definitely not a

---

[213] Schama, 2001 p. 226

[214] Lenman, 2004 p. 482

[215] Schama, 2001 p. 321

[216] Heywood, 2003 pp. 39-40

good thing politically or socially, and the consequences of weakness can be profound. Such governments can be prone to collapse, either being replaced by absolutist regimes or precipitating a return to the state of nature. Strong government according to Hobbes was the key not only for maintaining social and political order, it was also important for the intellectual, material, and technological progress of humanity. It did not matter how advanced any particular country and its society had become. For once its government had become weakened, or was overthrown, it would not take long to revert back to a chaotic situation very similar to how Hobbes believed the state of nature had been like.[217] There was certainly no room for believing that the state of nature was to be admired, or copied, as humanity had only progressed due to the presence of governments, laws, and moral values, all of which were absent from the state of nature.[218]

Interestingly enough Hobbes argued that the state of nature was ended when governments in individual countries were established, with the new perspective that the foundations of governance rested upon a contractual agreement between the people and the government. Thus Hobbes contended that agreement between the governments and the people were concluded through the use of social contract theory. Under social contracts governments pledged that they would maintain law and order, ensure that their people could adequately provide for themselves, and defend their country from any internal or external threats to security. The government was responsible for preventing any catastrophic reversions to the state of nature, and therefore could be justified in taking all steps that were deemed necessary. In return for being protected, and nurtured, people owed their governments absolute obedience, as disobedience led to the awful prospects of rebellions, civil wars, or worst of all a reversion back to the state of nature.[219]

---

[217] Heywood, 2003 p.39

[218] Eatwell & Wright, 2003 p. 72

[219] Heywood, 2003 p. 77

In the Second Treatise of Government, Locke would also regard social contract theory as vital for understanding how the state of nature operated, then subsequently how its members freely decided to end that state of nature by establishing governments to run their states.[220] Unlike Hobbes, Locke believed that although people agreed to a social contract they did that through making a rational choice that such a contract was best for them. However that choice is not eternally binding for the descendants of those that agreed to it originally.[221] People are only liable to obey their governments whilst a majority of the population regard those governments as holding legitimate authority.[222] Locke believed that governments had basic functions such as ensuring law and order, administering justice, and defending their countries. Apart from those functions governments had no need and no right to interfere in peoples' lives.[223] Governments did not have absolute authority to do anything, their people are free to renounce their social contract, and appoint new governments as required, even if at the cost of temporary return to a state of nature.[224] Locke's was unconcerned about a temporary return to the state of nature; it was better than Hobbes insistence on obeying tyrannical regimes. His argument that regime change was acceptable in certain circumstances was a truly revolutionary concept. It provided an intellectual defence of the Glorious Revolution, as well as providing rational arguments for subsequent revolutionaries.[225] Regimes could avoid been overthrown and a return to a state of nature by serving the needs of their people. In that they retained legitimacy and the people were well -governed.[226]

In some respects the differences between Locke and Hobbes over the notions of the state of nature are due to a difference of emphasis. They agreed that the state of nature was the starting point for societies that needed to progress to the formation of government and laws. Both men used their books to forward the social contract theory as the theoretical means of ending the state of nature. Social

---

[220]Heywood, 2003 p. 77

[221]Heywood, 2003 p. 77

[222]Heywood, 2000 p. 29

[223]Eatwell & Wright, 2003 p. 36

[224]Lenman, 2004 p. 482

[225]Schama, 2001 p. 321

[226]Heywood, 2000 p. 29

contracts allow people to have better lives than in a state of nature, as governments ensure stability and progress by passing laws and maintaining order. Both men believed that governments should be obeyed, Hobbes argued under all circumstances whilst Locke argued in all but the most exceptional circumstances. Hobbes emphasis on governments being able to use any means to keep hold of power and prevent a return to a state of nature was in sharp contrast to Locke's belief that rebellion was acceptable to prevent tyranny. Despite that difference Hobbes was only advocating authoritarian measures, and Locke was only advocating rebellion in extreme circumstances and not as a matter of course. The state was the supreme adjudicator of civil and legal disputes, and if it did that task properly it was better than the state of nature was.[227]

To conclude there were various differences between Locke and Hobbes when they presented their notions of the state of nature in the Second Treatise of Government, and the Leviathan. Hobbes took a less optimistic view of human nature than Locke did, which, can be explained by their different life experiences. Hobbes was already middle-aged by the time that Charles I poor relationship with Parliament resulted in the English Civil Wars, and the eventual overthrow of the monarchy. Hobbes compared the disorder, chaos, and civil war of his times with an imagined state of nature so that he could call on his contemporaries to obey their governments. Hobbes developed social contract theory to explain how the state of nature had been replaced by the rule of law. The state of nature, just like societies that rejected their governments was untenable as a means of sustaining stability or future political and economic development. Locke's notions relating to the state of nature were not as negative as those of Hobbes were as he had not had such strong experiences of the English Civil Wars. Locke continued Hobbes's use of social contract theory yet amended it to suit his notions of the state of nature. Social contracts may have ended the state of nature, but that state itself was not intrinsically bad, although it limited the pace of human development. The social contract was agreed to rationally and was not eternally binding, whilst a rebellion might bring a reversion to conditions like the state of nature providing it was only

---

[227]Heywood, 2003 pp. 39-40

temporary it would cause any damage to society. Thus for Locke the state of nature was ended by social contracts as governments and laws that should allow improvements. However tyrannical government was not better than the state of nature, and justified rebellion.

Bibliography

Comfort N (1993) Brewer's Politics, a phrase and fable dictionary, Cassell, London

Crystal D, (1998) The Cambridge Biographical Encyclopedia – 2nd edition, Cambridge University Press, Cambridge and New York

Eatwell R & Wright A, (2003) Contemporary Political Ideologies 2nd Edition, Continuum, London

Heywood A, (2001) Key Concepts in Politics, MacMillan, Basingstoke

Heywood A, (2003) Political Ideologies – An Introduction, 3rd edition, Palgrave MacMillan, Basingstoke

Lacey R, (2006) Great Tales from English History, the Battle of the Boyne to DNA, Little Brown, London

Lenman B P (2004) Chambers Dictionary of World History 2nd edition, Chambers, Edinburgh

Royale T, (2004) Civil War – The Wars of the Three Kingdoms 1638-1660, Abacus, London

Schama S, (2001) A History of Britain - The British Wars 1603-1776, BBC Worldwide, London

Vale B, (2006) A History of the Church of England 1529 – 1662, Amazon Kindle

Section 6

Outcomes of the English Civil Wars and Leading Figures

Parliamentary victory

The main outcome of the English Civil Wars was a parliamentary victory, though it was a strange kind of victory. After three distinct civil wars the New Model Army and Oliver Cromwell were in charge of the British Isles, yet they could not find a way to effectively govern the Three Republics, or the Commonwealth as it was termed. The Long Parliament was it thought the most important institution in Britain after the execution of Charles I and the declaration of a republic. The members of the Long Parliament argued amongst themselves while Cromwell and the New Model Army conducted brutal and highly effective campaigns in Ireland and Scotland. The stunning victory at Worcester in September 1651 brought the fighting to an end yet the squabbling at Westminster continued. Cromwell left his son Henry in charge of Ireland, cowered for the time being after the bloody sieges of Drogheda and Limerick.

Oliver Cromwell lost patience with the Rump Parliament, shutting it down in 1653 and replacing it with the Barebones Parliament. Unlike, Charles I he shut down Parliament without any opposition. He refused the offer of been made the king, and instead became Lord Protector until his death on 3 September 1658.

A United British State

For the period of the interregnum the British Isles were effectively controlled as a single United British state. This state was basically held together by Oliver Cromwell with his son Henry having a tight grip over Ireland after his father returned to England.

Yet after the restoration of the monarchy the three kingdoms went back to how they were before the wars began.

However there were politicians at Westminster that favoured a unitary structure with England dominating the rest of the British Isles.

A Constitutional Monarchy

The Lord Protectorate dragged on for another two years under Richard Cromwell, a man not capable of the brutality or the quick thinking of his father. By 1660 some members of the Lord Protectorate decided that the only solution for stability was to restore the monarchy, with Charles II taking his father's crowns. The difference was that it was a constitutional monarchy, in which the English Parliament held the most power. Charles II was content to sign the Breda Agreement to end his exile, and stayed on the throne until his death in 1685, though his younger brother James II (VII of Scotland) would lose his throne three years later.

John Pym

The Puritan John Pym was born in the county of Somerset during the year 1584.

Pym received a sound grammer school education, and was brought up as a Puritan. The Pym family were part of a network of hardline Protestants, which also happened to include the Cromwells.

Despite failing to leave the University of Oxford without a formal degree he went to London to start a legal career. However once in London he got drawn into politics, his Puritan beliefs placing him amongst the opposition to the absolutist ideas of the Stuart monarchy. Pym became an MP in 1614, when Parliament was increasingly less willing to do what James I wanted it to do.

James' problems with Parliament were nothing to compared to those of his son Charles I. Pym was amongst the most ardent opponents of the king, and was regarded by the government as a trouble maker. During the eleven years without a Parliament he remained stridently opposed to Charles I.

Pym was a prominent figure in the events leading up to the English Civil Wars, and Charles' failed attempt to arrest him and four other hard liners was the final straw for many.

He greatly assisted the Parliamentary victory by sealing the alliance with the Scots shortly before his death in 1643.

Robert Blake English Admiral and Soldier

Robert Blake was born in 1599 near Taunton in the county of Somerset, in the same year as his future ruler Oliver Cromwell. Blake was gifted academically and as his family were modestly wealthy he could afford to study at the University of Oxford. His life had been nothing out of the ordinary until after he turned forty in 1639.

As a member of the English gentry Blake was able to stand for Parliamentary elections in 1640 when Charles I inability to defeat the Scots in the Bishops War led to the calling of the Short Parliament, in which Blake was elected for Taunton. He was strongly linked to the Parliamentary cause, and was also a MP for the same seat in the Long Parliament before the start of the English Civil Wars.

Blake served the Parliamentary army well, proving to be a capable commander, he showed his skill with his command of the garrison of Taunton against numerically superior Royalist forces in 1645. Blake was considered to be a reliable commander within the New Model Army. After the execution of Charles I the Rump Parliament decided to appoint as an Admiral in the New Model Navy tasked with defeating Prince Rupert who was raiding Commonwealth shipping from Dutch and Portuguese bases. The appointment was an inspired one, Blake was an efficient soldier but he turned out to be an exceptional admiral. Besides defeating the Royalists the Commonwealth would go on to fight wars against both the Dutch Republic and Spain.

Blake played a leading role in defeating Prince Rupert and securing control of home waters for the New Model Navy. Defeating the Dutch was a much greater achievement as their navy was the best in the world up to that point. Blake led the English ships that defeated the Dutch off Portland in 1654. He would later defeat the Spanish, capture one of their treasure fleets, sink another one, and then mastermind the capture of Jamaica in 1657.

Robert Blake died at sea shortly after taking Jamaica, having played his part in making the English navy a formidable fighting force when it became the Royal Navy again.

Henry Ireton

Ireton was a leading New Model Army officer and the son in law of Oliver Cromwell (marrying Elizabeth Cromwell in 1646). He made his name from serving in the cavalry and as a hard line opponent of the monarchy, being one of the regicides.

Henry Ireton was second in command when the New Model Army went to Ireland, with Oliver Cromwell being in command after Fairfax refused to go. He was made Lord Deputy of Ireland in 1650 and died the following year of the bubonic plague during the long drawn siege of Limerick.
Ireton was replaced as Lord Deputy in Ireland by Henry Cromwell.

Edward Montagu (Second Earl of Manchester)

At the start of the First Civil War, Montagu was in charge of the Parliamentary forces alongside the Earl of Essex. Their tactics were not as effective as those of Cromwell or Fairfax, meaning that Montagu concentrated on politics after 1645. He became the Speaker of the House of Lords and was a notable backer of the Restoration.

Prince Rupert

Prince Rupert of the Palatine was the nephew of Charles I and was born in 1619. Rupert was the third son of Elizabeth Stuart and Frederick V, the Elector Palatine.

He was a capable cavalry commander and could have won the battle of Edgehill in 1642 yet did not regroup his troops allowing the Parliamentary forces to recover. Rupert and his forces did not have the same tactical ability as either Thomas Fairfax or Oliver Cromwell. He was well beaten at Marston Moor and Naseby before surrendering the garrison at Bristol.

Robert Devereux (Earl of Essex)

Devereux succeeded his executed father as Earl of Essex in 1604. Unlike his father, Robert was a serious minded Protestant soldier and statesman, though his public reputation was tarnished after his wife divorced him in 1613. He was originally loyal servant to James I and Charles I.

Devereux was even second in command of the ineffective campaign against the Scots in the Bishop's War of 1639. As the Three

Kingdoms moved towards war, Essex opted to become a Parliamentary commander. He led the war effort in conjunction with the Earl of Manchester before the emergence of Thomas Fairfax and Oliver Cromwell. He stepped down from command prior to the passing of the Self-Denying Ordinance and died in 1646.

Thomas Fairfax

Thomas Fairfax was born in Yorkshire during1612. He was the son of Fernando Lord Fairfax.

At the beginning of the English Civil Wars, Thomas Fairfax and his father decided to raise a regiment to fight for Parliament by recruiting men in the West Riding of Yorkshire..

The Fairfax regiment would eventually be part of the New Model Army, arguably the most potent army in the era of the civil wars. He distinguished himself at Marston Moor and then Naseby. That is why he was made head of the New Model Army. Fairfax did not support the execution of Charles I.

In 1649 Fairfax did not go to Ireland so Oliver Cromwell and Henry Ireton went instead. He later stepped down rather than the fight the Scots, so Cromwell won the victories at Dunbar and Worcester.

In 1660 he went to Breda to arrange the return of Charles II, and kept out of the limelight until his death in 1671.

Bibliography

Crystal D (1998) The Cambridge Biographical Encyclopedia, Cambridge University Press
Gardiner J & Wenborn N (1995) The History Today Companion to British History, Collins & Brown, London

Holmes R (2007) Battlefield – Decisive Conflicts in History, Oxford University Press, Oxford

Kennedy P (1976) The Rise and fall of British Naval Mastery, Penguin, London
Lenman B (2004) Chambers Dictionary of World History,

Chambers, Edinburgh

Printed in Great Britain
by Amazon